OCCASIONAL PAPER 263

Macroeconomic Implications of Financial Dollarization

The Case of Uruguay

Edited by Marco Piñón, Gaston Gelos, and Alejandro López-Mejía

INTERNATIONAL MONETARY FUND
Washington DC
2008

Production: IMF Multimedia Services Division
Typesetting: Alicia Etchebarne-Bourdin
Figures: Andrew Sylvester

Cataloging-in-Publication Data

Macroeconomic implications of financial dollarization: the case of Uruguay/ edited by Marco Piñón, Gaston Gelos, and Alejandro López-Mejía— Washington, D.C.: International Monetary Fund, 2008.

p. cm.—(Occasional paper, 0251-6365; 263)

Includes bibliographical references.
ISBN 978-1-58906-727-1

1. Dollarization—Uruguay. 2. Monetary policy—Uruguay. 3. Banks and banking—Uruguay. 4. Finance—Uruguay. I. Piñón, Marco. II. Gelos, Gaston. III. López-Mejía, Alejandro. IV. International Monetary Fund. V. Occasional paper (International Monetary Fund); no. 263.

HG905 .M337 2008

Please send orders to:
International Monetary Fund, Publication Services
700 19th Street, N.W., Washington, D.C. 20431, U.S.A.
Tel.: (202) 623-7430 Fax: (202) 623-7201
E-mail: publications@imf.org
Internet: www.imfbookstore.org

Contents

Preface vii

Abbreviations ix

I Overview **1**
Marco Piñón

Monetary Policy in a Dollarized Economy 1
External Linkages Under Dollarization 2
Financial Vulnerabilities and Insurance Mechanisms 3

Part 1. Monetary Policy in a Dollarized Economy

II Inflation Process in Uruguay **7**
Gaston Gelos and Fernanda Rossi Iriondo

Inflation Dynamics and Inflation Expectations 7
Determinants of Inflation Expectations 10
Conclusions 13
Appendix 2.1. Cointegration Tests, Bivariate Vector Error Correction Model, and Tests of Efficiency of Inflation Forecasts 14
Bibliography 16

III Pass-Through, Dollarization, and Credibility in Uruguay **17**
Alejandro López-Mejía, Alessandro Rebucci, and Carolina Saizar

Background 17
Has Pass-Through Declined in Uruguay? 20
Is Monetary Policy Credibility Linked to Financial Dollarization? 22
Conclusions 24
Appendix 3.1. Measuring Credibility 25
Bibliography 25

Part 2. External Linkages Under Dollarization

IV Role of Bank Lending in the Transmission of Macroeconomic Shocks **29**
Gaston Gelos and Marco Piñón

Descriptive Evidence on the Importance of Bank Lending for Economic Activity 30
Banks' Response to Shocks: Microeconomic Evidence 30
Conclusions 33
Bibliography 33

V What Is the Degree of Competition Intensity in the Uruguayan Banking System? 34
Gaston Gelos and Marco Piñón

Assessing the Degree of Competition 35
Conclusions 37
Bibliography 37

VI What Drives Uruguayan Sovereign Spreads? The Role of Global Factors and Regional Spillovers 39
Gustavo Adler and Stephanie Eble

Stylized Facts 39
What Drives Sovereign Spreads? 43
Conclusions 47
Bibliography 47

Part 3. Financial Vulnerabilities and Insurance Mechanisms

VII Has the Uruguayan Financial System Become More Resilient to Shocks? An Analysis Adapting the Merton Framework to a Country Without Equity Market Data 51
Marcos Rietti Souto

Merton Framework 51
Stress Tests 52
Modified Merton Framework 53
Conclusions 56
Appendix 7.1. Estimating Risk Indicators for the Corporate and Banking Sectors 57
Bibliography 59

VIII Optimal Level of Reserves in Financially Dollarized Economies: The Case of Uruguay 60
Fernando M. Gonçalves

Vulnerabilities and the Role of Reserves in Uruguay 60
Optimal Level of Reserves 62
Sensitivity Analysis 65
Conclusions 67
Appendix 8.1. A Model of Optimal Reserve Levels in Financially Dollarized Economies 67
Appendix 8.2. Level of Reserves Required to Cover a 2002-Like Crisis 69
Bibliography 69

Figures

2.1. Actual and 12-Month-Ahead Expected Inflation 8
2.2. Recursive Coefficient Equation (1) (Recursive ordinary least squares estimates) 9
2.3. Determinants of Inflationary Expectations: Recursive Coefficients 11
2.4. Twelve-Month-Ahead Expected Inflation: Actual Versus Fitted (Generalized method of moments–based model) 12
2.5. Recursive Estimates of Coefficient on Inflation Target (Recursive ordinary least squares estimates) 12
2.6. Dispersion of Inflation Forecasts 13

3.1. Inflation in Uruguay 18
3.2. Nominal Exchange Rate and Foreign Exchange Rate Intervention 19
3.3. A Measure of Financial Sector Development 20
3.4. Pass-Through Rolling Regression Coefficients 21
3.5. Deposit Dollarization 22
3.6. Credit Dollarization 22
3.7. A Measure of Credibility 23
3.8. Financial Dollarization and Credibility 24
3.9. Impulse Response Functions 24
4.1. Bank Lending in Uruguay 29
4.2. Correlations Between Leads and Lags of the Cyclical Components of Credit and GDP 31
5.1. Bank Credit to the Private Sector in Selected Countries 34
5.2. Concentration Index 35
6.1. Uruguay, Latin America and Global Emerging Markets Bond Index (EMBI) Spreads, 1996–2006 40
6.2. Country Fundamentals and External Factors, 1996–2006 41
6.3. Selected Country Spreads and Latin American Emerging Markets Bond Index (EMBI) Spread, Pre– and Post–Uruguayan Crisis 42
6.4. Standard & Poor's Credit Rating for Selected Latin American Countries, 1996–2006 44
6.5. Uruguay and Selected Latin American Country Spreads, Pre- and Postcrisis 45
7.1. Merton Framework 52
7.2. Liquidity Ratios After Stress Shocks 53
7.3. Capital Adequacy Ratio (Percentage of Risk-Weighted Assets) After Stress Shocks 54
7.4. Expected Losses Given Default in the Corporate Sector 55
7.5. Banking Sector Default Probability 56
7.6. Relationship Between Assets and Asset Volatility in Uruguay 56
7.7. Default Probabilities: A Scenario Analysis 57
7A.1. Uruguay's Corporate Sector: Components of Distance to Distress 58
7A.2. Uruguay's Banking Sector Volatilities 59
8.1. Financial Account Reversal, Dollar Deposits, and Reserves in Uruguay 61
8.2. Short-Term Foreign Currency Debt and Foreign Currency Deposits in Uruguay 61
8.3. Withdrawal of Foreign Currency Deposits in 2002 62
8.4. Benchmark Measures of Reserve Adequacy 62
8.5. Optimal Versus Actual Level of Reserves in Uruguay 65
8.6. Actual and Implied Reserves 65
8.7. Sensitivity Analysis 66

Tables

2.1. Consumer Price Index Inflation Regressions with Survey Data 8
2.2. Determinants of Inflation Expectations 10
2.3. Tests of Unbiasedness of Inflation Forecasts 14
2A.1. Johansen Cointegration Test Results 14
2A.2. Adjustment Coefficients in a Bivariate Vector Error Correction on Actual and Expected Inflation 15
2A.3. Tests of Efficiency of Inflation Forecasts 15
3.1. Short- and Long-Run Exchange Rate Pass-Through, Selected Countries 21
4.1. Financing Structure of Firms in Uruguay, 2004 30
4.2. Selected Indicators of Uruguayan Banks by Type, 2006 31
4.3. Differential Response of Local Currency Loan Growth to Monetary Policy Shocks by Bank Characteristic 32

4.4. Differential Response of Foreign Currency Loan Growth to Foreign Shocks 33
5.1. Panzar and Rosse's *H* Statistic 36
5.2. Results from Revenue Estimations 36
6.1. Sovereign Spread Correlation, Pre- and Postcrisis 43
6.2. Pairwise Granger Causality Tests 44
6.3. Unit Root Test: Augmented Dickey-Fuller (ADF) 46
6.4. Variance Decomposition 47
7.1. 2006 Financial Sector Assessment Program: Stress Tests Assumption 53
7.2. Total Government Assistance to Banks 55
8.1. Variable Parameters 63
8.2. Fixed Parameters 63
8.3. Implicit Parameters 67

The following conventions are used in this publication:

- In tables, a blank cell indicates "not applicable," ellipsis points (. . .) indicate "not available," and 0 or 0.0 indicates "zero" or "negligible." Minor discrepancies between sums of constituent figures and totals are due to rounding.
- An en dash (–) between years or months (for example, 2005–06 or January–June) indicates the years or months covered, including the beginning and ending years or months; a slash or virgule (/) between years or months (for example, 2005/06) indicates a fiscal or financial year, as does the abbreviation FY (for example, FY2006).
- "Billion" means a thousand million; "trillion" means a thousand billion.
- "Basis points" refer to hundredths of 1 percentage point (for example, 25 basis points are equivalent to ¼ of 1 percentage point).

As used in this publication, the term "country" does not in all cases refer to a territorial entity that is a state as understood by international law and practice. As used here, the term also covers some territorial entities that are not states but for which statistical data are maintained on a separate and independent basis.

Preface

In recent years, the International Monetary Fund has set itself the challenge of becoming a global center of excellence on international finance and its linkages with broader macroeconomic phenomenons, including growth, inflation, investment, currency values, and overall stability.

The analytical work brought together here is a good example of this new emphasis. It parallels the shift in the IMF's relationship with Uruguay, which has moved on from dealing with the aftermath of the 2002 crisis to understanding underlying economic structures and transmission mechanisms in a heavily dollarized financial system, and bringing to the fore related policy issues. The questions posed in this volume are central to the conduct of macroeconomic policy: How much room to maneuver does the central bank of a dollarized financial system have to influence inflation expectations and dynamics? Through what channels is monetary policy transmitted, and what effect does policy credibility have on the degree of dollarization? What level of international reserves is prudent?

I would like to thank all concerned for their contributions, including the Uruguayan authorities.

The opinions expressed in this paper are solely those of its authors and do not necessarily reflect the views of the International Monetary Fund, its Executive Directors, or national authorities.

Anoop Singh
Director
Western Hemisphere Department
International Monetary Fund

Abbreviations

BHU	Banco Hipotecario del Uruguay
BROU	Banco de la República Oriental del Uruguay
CAR	Capital adequacy ratio
CPI	Consumer price index
EDP	Expected default probability
EMBI	Emerging Markets Bond Index (JPMorgan)
FIML	Full-information maximum likelihood
FSAP	Financial Sector Assessment Program (IMF)
GDP	Gross domestic product
GMM	Generalized method of moments
HH	Herfindahl-Hirschman
LIBOR	London Interbank Offered Rate
NPV	Net present value
OLS	Ordinary least squares
PPI	Producer price index
UBI	Uruguayan Bond Index
VAR	Vector autoregression
VEC	Vector error correction
VIX	Volatility Index (Chicago Board Options Exchange)

I Overview

Marco Piñón

This paper assesses the implications of high financial dollarization for macroeconomic policies and vulnerabilities in Uruguay. Dollarization creates balance sheet exposure to exchange rate changes and poses important policy questions. Understanding the exposures of different sectors and the transmission of macroeconomic shocks is key to determine appropriate policies and instruments. To shed light on these issues, the paper assesses the scope for an independent monetary policy and for the exchange rate to be a shock absorber in a financially dollarized economy, the transmission of shocks by the financial system and the role of external factors in explaining key financial variables, and balance sheet vulnerabilities and the need for insurance mechanisms.

The analysis is particularly relevant at this juncture, as Uruguay pursues key postcrisis monetary and financial reforms. The country has experienced a remarkable recovery after the 2002 crisis, supported by sound policies and favorable external conditions. With the framework put in place in 2002, Uruguay abandoned an exchange rate peg in favor of a free float, adopted a monetary regime initially based on money targets, improved financial prudential norms and supervision, and accumulated significant central bank reserves. Since then, the dollarization of the banking system has declined, but it is still high. Against this background, the country now faces issues beyond those addressed to stabilize the economy. The analysis has a direct bearing on the ongoing efforts to move toward a fully fledged inflation-targeting regime and develop interest rates as monetary instruments as well as other related issues, including the preparedness of the financial system to deal with shocks and the adequacy of current central bank reserves.

The main findings can be broadly summarized as follows:

- Despite high financial dollarization, there is scope for domestic monetary policy to be effective. Beyond the direct impact of the monetary stance, with increased credibility, particularly during the periods when the exchange rate has been allowed to float, the central bank has been able to influence inflation through the expectation channel. In addition, banks' lending behavior suggests that there is a limited but strengthening bank lending channel for monetary policy.
- A flexible exchange rate can be an effective absorber of external shocks in Uruguay. With a partial and declining pass-through, exchange rate movements can help restore balances and deal with shocks. At the same time, instruments other than the exchange rate, such as interest rates, are likely to be more appropriate to manage monetary policy as Uruguay gradually moves toward a fully fledged inflation-targeting framework.
- External financial developments play a substantial role in Uruguay, partly because of high dollarization. Beyond the still significant real linkages to the region and nonresident deposits in the financial system, there are several other important financial links with the rest of the world. In particular, banks' dollar lending is found to be influenced by U.S. monetary policy. Also, sovereign spreads behavior suggests that investors link Uruguay's fortunes to a considerable extent to external developments.
- Sustaining sound policies over the medium term will be essential to further increase the effectiveness of policy instruments and reduce spillover risks. Despite much progress, there are still vulnerabilities and policy constraints imposed by dollarization. A clear monetary framework and commitment to the inflation objectives, within a flexible exchange rate regime, appear important to further increase central bank credibility and reduce real costs of lowering inflation. In due time, this could also assist in lowering dollarization. Continued progress toward regaining investment grade would likely go a long way in reducing external linkages. Although nearing appropriate levels, further reserve accumulation would also be desirable.

This work explores the implications of financial dollarization in seven papers, presented in three main sections.

Monetary Policy in a Dollarized Economy

Uruguay remains a highly dollarized economy, potentially limiting the scope for monetary policy.

Under outright dollarization, monetary policy is generally expected to play little or no role. In Uruguay, however, although financial dollarization is among the highest in the world, the peso is the basis for most transactions and contracts in the economy. Thus, the question of whether there is scope for monetary policy is an empirical issue:

- Gelos and Rossi Iriondo study the determinants and dynamics of inflation and explore the expectation channel of monetary policy. With higher-than-targeted inflation, lowering inflation has become among the authorities' top short-term policy concerns. The study establishes econometrically that forward-looking expectations have been the key drivers of inflation, particularly since the adoption of a flexible exchange rate. This is an important insight because it suggests that inflation could be lowered without large economic activity costs. It also shows that the central bank has been gaining credibility, with announced inflation targets playing an increasing role in forming expectations. Fiscal variables, in turn, are among the factors explaining expectations. Monetary aggregates become important only after the adoption of a flexible exchange rate regime over longer-term horizon forecasts.

- López-Mejía, Rebucci, and Saizar assess the exchange rate pass-through to domestic prices and the effectiveness of a flexible exchange rate as a shock absorber and indirect channel of transmission of monetary policy. The authors show that the pass-through began to decline as early as 1994–95 but has become unstable since late 2005. This result suggests that the exchange rate has become a less effective nominal anchor. Thus, the role of an appreciation in offsetting inflationary pressures, although still important, has decreased. It also means that the exchange rate can generate expenditure switching effects, helping isolate the economy from shocks. Using an innovative Bayesian approach, the study also provides further evidence that monetary policy credibility has generally increased, giving the central bank larger scope to conduct monetary policy effectively. However, in contrast with Gelos and Rossi Iriondo, who found a steady increase in credibility, this study suggests a moderate decline between 2006 and mid-2007. The research also finds that increased credibility could lower dollarization, although long periods of time may be needed.

A further aspect to assess the scope for monetary policy is whether there exists a credit channel for monetary policy in Uruguay. To the extent that banks' lending reacts to monetary policy changes, the scope and effectiveness of monetary policy would be enhanced. This discussion is presented in the second section as part of a more comprehensive study of banks' lending behavior, going beyond the credit channel.

External Linkages Under Dollarization

Given the importance of external developments for a small, open, and dollarized economy, this part assesses key aspects of Uruguay's financial linkages with the rest of the world. The country has made significant strides in reducing vulnerabilities associated with external developments. For example, nonresident deposits in the banking system, which were at the center of the 2002 crisis, have been halved as a share of total deposits, and exports have become geographically more diversified. Still, banks' balance sheets are likely to be affected by changes in U.S. monetary conditions, given their substantial holdings of U.S. financial assets and, more generally, the high degree of dollarization of their operations. Moreover, in line with other middle-income economies, global and emerging market conditions appear to have become more important in recent years.

- Gelos and Piñón analyze the transmission of macroeconomic shocks by the domestic banking system. Relying on detailed microeconomic data, they exploit the time series and cross-section dimensions of the data to draw inferences on banks' behavior. The transmission of domestic monetary policy changes, an issue more related to the previous section, is studied here within a single framework for domestic and external shocks. The results suggest a limited but growing lending channel for monetary policy, with banks decreasing or increasing peso lending as domestic monetary conditions tighten or loosen, respectively. A similar transmission of foreign shocks is found, with banks adjusting dollar lending to changes in U.S. interest rates. Supporting the hypothesis on the role of financial frictions in the behavior of banks, the effects are stronger for less liquid and less capitalized banks. Thus, as the share of peso lending continues to increase, the impact of monetary policy will become stronger. That said, with dollar lending still representing the largest share, external shocks remain key determinants of bank lending.

- In a second study, Gelos and Piñón examine the competitive conditions of the Uruguayan banking system. This is important not only to assess prospects for increased financial intermediation, but also because imperfect competition may propagate external shocks and amplify swings (Mandelman, 2006). Using techniques from the new empirical industrial organizations approach (Panzar and Rose methodology), the study concludes that the degree of competition is relatively low by international standards. This raises the challenge of strengthening competition intensity without endangering financial stability. (See Chapter V for full references.)

- Adler and Eble assess the importance of external factors in driving Uruguayan sovereign spreads. Their study concludes that, although fundamentals explain part of the variation in sovereign spreads, external factors play a key role and have become more important since the 2002 financial crisis. Furthermore, although Uruguay was largely insulated from regional and emerging market economy shocks—and perceived as a safe haven in the region—until the crisis, its spreads have since moved closely with those of neighboring countries. Econometric estimates suggest that investors' perceptions of Uruguay's financial interdependencies were revised significantly following the crisis, and that the downgrading of Uruguay to speculative grade in 2002 heightened financial spillovers and global and regional linkages. Thus, against the background of recent upgrades in credit ratings, it will be important to sustain appropriate policies to continue making strides toward regaining investment-grade status.

Financial Vulnerabilities and Insurance Mechanisms

This section evaluates vulnerabilities and insurance mechanisms in place against potential balance of payments or bank deposit withdrawal shocks. Commercial banks' soundness and liquidity indicators have improved substantially since the 2002 crisis, with higher profitability, capital adequacy, and liquid foreign assets, and lower exposure to nonresident deposits. At the same time, central bank reserves have increased substantially. However, although vulnerabilities have clearly declined, high dollarization poses important risks. Thus, there is still a need to assess the capacity of the banking system and of the economy as a whole to cope with external shocks and the adequacy of protective mechanisms, particularly the level of central bank reserves. The studies in this section include the following:

- Rietti Souto examines banking system vulnerabilities from the perspective of balance sheet exposures, asset volatility, and default probabilities. First, an update of the stress tests undertaken by the 2006 Financial Sector Stability Assessment (FSSA) confirms that, with the exception of extreme events, the banking system would be resilient to most shocks. Severe external current and capital account shock scenarios, such as a sudden stop, illustrate remaining vulnerabilities, but also a significantly less severe impact on the banking system than in 2002. Second, as a novel approach, the contingent claims (or Merton's framework) are adapted to a case without equity markets, using monthly balance sheet data of individual banks. Although lacking market values, a central feature of Merton's framework, the results track the 2002 crisis well, displaying significant asset value volatility. Consistent with the FSSA's results, the findings suggest that banks' resilience to shocks has increased significantly since the 2002 crisis. Estimated default probabilities resulting from a simulated 2002-like shock, although important, are about half the estimated level for 2002.

- Gonçalves assesses the adequacy of foreign reserves as insurance against balance of payments and banking crises. Jeanne and Ranciere's model for optimal reserves is extended by explicitly incorporating the dollarization of bank deposits. The model studies reserve levels from the perspective of consumption-smoothing benefits against the quasi-fiscal costs of holding reserves. The results indicate that reserves are nearing optimal levels, given a sharply improved debt profile away from short-term, reduced nonresident deposits, and substantial liquidity held by banks. Nonetheless, further reserve accumulation is desirable going forward. As the recovery matures and lending picks up, banks' liquidity would likely decline and higher reserves would be needed from a prudential perspective. Moreover, higher levels would also be useful for crisis prevention, beyond the crisis mitigation objective taken into account in the framework.

Part I

Monetary Policy in a Dollarized Economy

II Inflation Process in Uruguay

Gaston Gelos and Fernanda Rossi Iriondo

Following chronic high inflation, Uruguay reduced inflation gradually through a disinflation program in the 1990s, reaching single digits by 1998. Inflation has since remained moderate, except for an outburst during the 2002 financial crisis and devaluation. In that year, the country moved to a flexible exchange rate regime, and inflation began declining quickly to low single digits by 2005. It has since increased somewhat to about 8 percent.

With relatively high inflation vis-à-vis the region and other emerging markets, a relevant question is how costly it would be to reduce it further. Various aspects of the factors driving inflation in Uruguay remain to be understood better. First, what is the degree of inflation persistence, and to what extent is inflation driven by backward-looking behavior and expectations? Understanding this is important for the conduct of monetary policy: with much backward-looking behavior, temporary inflationary shocks tend to persist and the output costs of reducing inflation quickly are higher. Second, what are the determinants of inflation expectations? This question is relevant given the monetary authorities' increased focus on the inflation objective, de-emphasizing monetary targets. In such a context, anchoring expectations is a precondition for a successful monetary policy.

This chapter explores the dynamics of inflation in Uruguay, making use of survey data, focusing on the role of inflation expectations and their determinants. First, it assesses the role of inflation expectations in shaping the inflation process by estimating a New Keynesian Phillips curve. Second, it explores the determinants of survey expectations. Third, it discusses the rationality of survey expectations.

The chapter finds that expectations are more important than lagged inflation in shaping the inflation process, suggesting that inertia is relatively small. The importance of lagged inflation decreased with the adoption of a flexible exchange rate and has remained low since then. The results also suggest that, in addition to marginal cost proxies, fiscal variables are important in explaining expectations. There is some evidence that the central bank has gained credibility, with announced inflation targets playing an increasing role in forming expectations. Survey expectations over a 12-month horizon are neither unbiased nor efficient, but 1-month-ahead inflation expectations appear to be rational.

Inflation Dynamics and Inflation Expectations

To assess the importance of inflation expectations, this chapter uses a structural price-setting model nesting two types of price-setting behavior (see Galí and Gertler, 1999; Celasun, Gelos, and Prati, 2004a and 2004b; and Celasun and McGettigan, 2005). Backward-looking price setters update the average new price based on the most recently observed inflation rate. Forward-looking price setters set prices based on their expectations, which may or may not be rational. The resulting inflation rate in period t equals

$$\pi_t = \alpha + \delta\pi_{t-1} + (1 - \delta)E_t\, \pi_{t+1} + \phi mc_t + \varepsilon_t, \qquad (1)$$

where π is the 12-month (or monthly) consumer price index (CPI) inflation rate, $E_t\pi_{t+1}$ is the expected inflation rate in 12 (or 1) month(s), π_{t-1} refers to inflation between 24 and 12 months ago (or between 2 and 1 months ago), and mc are marginal costs.

In the empirical work, annual inflation expectations from consensus forecasts are used. For comparison purposes, a shorter sample of monthly inflation expectations from a survey conducted since 2004 by the Uruguayan central bank is also used (Figure 2.1).[1,2] Because a typical firm in a small open economy is likely to use imported intermediate goods and domestic labor as inputs in production, a combination of the real effective exchange rate and domestic real unit labor costs (both in deviations from a linear trend) is used as a proxy of real marginal costs. Data for the period January 1998–September 2006 are used. To address poten-

[1]One-year-ahead inflation expectations are calculated as a weighted average of this year and next year's inflation forecast. Data are available on a monthly basis starting in 2001 and bimonthly prior to that. Data are interpolated for the missing months.

[2]Roberts (1995 and 1997) pioneered the use of survey expectations in estimating Phillips curves and inflation dynamics in the United States. Use in emerging markets is not widespread.

Figure 2.1. Actual and 12-Month-Ahead Expected Inflation

(In percent)

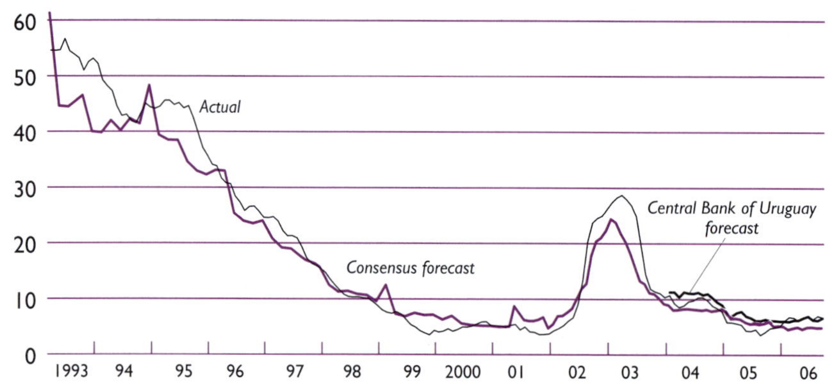

Source: IMF staff estimates.

Table 2.1. Consumer Price Index Inflation Regressions with Survey Data

Forecast Horizon	One Year				One Month			
Estimate	(1)	(2)	(3)	(4)	(5)	(6)	(7)	(8)
Constant	0.003	0.003	0.002	–0.031	0.001	–0.002	–0.001	–0.004
	(0.003)	(0.004)	(0.007)	(0.075)	(0.001)	(0.002)	(0.001)	(0.008)
Lagged inflation	–0.17	–0.08*	–0.032	–0.168	–0.18	–0.30*	–0.28*	–0.28
	(0.106)	(0.045)	(0.134)	(0.227)	(0.161)	(0.162)	(0.143)	(0.168)
Inflation forecast	1.17***	1.08***	1.032***	1.168***	1.18***	1.30***	1.28***	1.28***
	(0.106)	(0.045)	(0.134)	(0.227)	(0.161)	(0.162)	(0.143)	(0.168)
Real effective exchange rate gap	13.9***	0.879	—	—	—	6.12***	—	—
	(2.905)	(7.934)				(2.936)		
Real wage gap	—	–0.002*	—	—	0	0.001***	—	—
		(0.001)			0	0		
Output gap	—	—	–0.116**	—	—	—	–0.013	—
			(0.051)				(0.008)	
Unemployment rate	—	—	—	0.262	—	—	—	0.028
				(0.552)				(0.07)
Adjusted R^2	0.92	0.92	0.86	0.85	0.27	0.45	0.4	0.4
Sample	1998:01–2006:09				2004:01–2006:09			
Number of observations	105				33			
Source of inflationary expectations	consensus forecasts				Central Bank of Uruguay			

Source: IMF staff estimates.

Notes: Generalized method of moments (GMM) estimates. Andrews bandwidth standard errors are given in parentheses. For 12-month forecast horizon the instruments for lagged inflation were inflation (–2) in equations 1 and 4; 12-month exchange rate change (–2) in equation 3; and lagged inflation in equation 2. Oil prices inflation (–1) was used as instrument for inflation forecast. The other regressors were used as instruments in the remaining equations. For 1-month forecast horizon, equation 1 includes inflation forecast (–1) as instrument for inflation forecast. The other regressors were used as instruments in this and the remaining equations.

*, **, *** indicate significance at the 10, 5, and 1 percent level, respectively. — signifies a variable not included in the estimation.

Figure 2.2. Recursive Coefficient Equation (1)
(Recursive ordinary least squares estimates)
(Coefficient of lagged inflation and two standard error bands in equation 1)

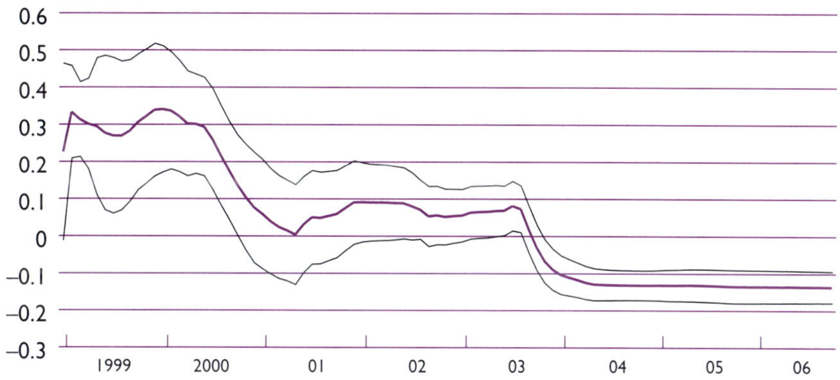

Source: IMF staff estimates.

tial endogeneity problems, the equation is estimated by the generalized method of moments (GMM). The equation is also estimated on a monthly forecast horizon for inflation forecasts for January 2004–September 2006 from a Central Bank of Uruguay survey.[3]

The results indicate that inflation expectations drive the inflation process (Table 2.1). In the case of annual inflation, the coefficient on expected future inflation is close to 1, whereas the coefficient on lagged inflation is insignificant in all but one case, where it is slightly negative. The real effective exchange rate enters the estimation with a statistically significant positive coefficient, in line with the notion that foreign prices are important in determining prices in Uruguay. Using monthly data, the role of expectations is even stronger. The coefficient on expected future inflation is larger than 1, whereas the coefficient on lagged inflation is negative and smaller. Proxy marginal costs enter the estimation significantly with positive coefficients, but a much smaller fraction of the monthly variation in inflation can be explained compared with the case of annual data. Table 2.1 shows estimations with the coefficients on lagged and expected inflation constrained to sum 1, as suggested by theory. The key results do not change when estimating the equations without restrictions.

Estimations allowing for the possibility of nonstationarity confirm the key results. With relatively short time series, the issue of possible nonstationarity is difficult to address given the low power of standard tests. Tests following Clemente, Montañés, and Reyes (1998) suggest the presence of a unit root even after allowing for two structural breaks (not shown). Thus, we also estimate a system using the FIML (full-information maximum-likelihood) method by Johansen and Swensen (1999), confirming a stationary relationship between inflation, expected inflation, and proxy variables of marginal costs. In line with the GMM results, the estimated coefficient on expected inflation was greater than 1 and significant. The proxies for marginal costs were positive but not statistically significant (not shown).

Recursive Estimates

A recursive estimation shows that the importance of lagged inflation has declined. Indeed, it falls sharply after the floating of the exchange rate, stabilizing after mid-2003 (Figure 2.2).

Inflation Persistence

The role of lagged inflation is limited, even after accounting for its impact on expectations and wage formation. If inflation expectations were largely driven by past inflation, the coefficient on lagged inflation would underestimate the overall role of past inflation in shaping the inflation process. To explore this issue, we re-estimated equation (1), replacing expected inflation with the residual of a regression of expected inflation on lagged inflation, finding that the coefficient does not change substantially. Similarly, backward-looking wage indexation may induce

[3]The monthly surveys conducted by the central bank are available from 2004.

inertia through the marginal cost variable, thus leading to underestimation of the importance of lagged inflation. Therefore, the residuals of a regression of unit labor costs on lagged inflation as marginal cost proxy are also used, without altering the qualitative results. All these factors point to low inflation inertia.

Determinants of Inflation Expectations

What factors explain inflation expectations? Because inflation expectations appear to be a key driving force of Uruguayan inflation dynamics, anchoring expectations is important for monetary policy. Following Celasun, Gelos, and Prati (2004a and 2004b), it is key to investigate the role of past inflation, fiscal outcomes, the exchange rate, monetary policy variables, and real wages on inflation expectations by estimating variants of the following general model:

$$\pi_t^e = \alpha_0 + \alpha_1\pi_{t-1} + \alpha_2 pb_{t-1} + \alpha_3 mc_{t-1} + \alpha_4 monetaryvariables_{t-1} + u_t, \quad (2)$$

Table 2.2. Determinants of Inflation Expectations

	Generalized Method of Moments Estimates							Cointegration Equation Estimates
Estimate	(1)	(2)	(3)	(4)	(5)	(6)	(7)	(8)
Constant	0.039*** (0.004)	0.042*** (0.004)	0.001 (0.026)	—	–0.11*** (0.039)	0.010*** (0.003)	—	0.03
Inflation (–1)	0.699*** (0.03)	0.662*** (0.029)	0.76*** (0.075)	0.76*** (0.067)	–0.064 (0.133)	0.240** (0.108)	0.243** (0.0943)	0.8 (0.086)
Inflation target (–1)	—	—	—	—	1.44*** (0.489)	—	—	—
Primary balance/GDP (–1)	–0.005*** (0.001)	–0.005*** (0.001)	–0.003** (0.002)	–0.003** (0.0015)	0.018*** (0.005)	–0.001** (0.001)	0.001*** 0	–0.012 (0.003)
Real effective exchange rate gap (–1)	12.96*** (3.32)	—	—	—	32.69*** (7.532)	1.510** (0.659)	1.550** (0.649)	60.02 (16.72)
Real wage gap (–1)	—	–0.002*** 0	—	—	—	—	—	0.005 (0.002)
Unemployment rate (–1)	—	—	0.19 (0.203)	0.20*** (0.039)	—	—	—	—
Year-on-year M1 growth (–1)	—	—	0.05 (0.038)	0.05 (0.034)	—	—	—	—
Year-on-year exchange rate change (–1)	—	—	–0.04* (0.022)	–0.04* (0.02)	—	—	—	—
DC	—	—	0.02* (0.015)	0.02** (0.011)	—	—	—	—
DP*Inflation (–1)	–0.243*** (0.035)	–0.216*** (0.026)	–0.18** (0.078)	–0.18*** (0.037)	—	—	—	—
Adjusted R^2	0.93	0.94	0.88	0.92	0.84	0.26	0.16	0.24
Forecasts horizon		12 months ahead			12 months ahead	1 month ahead		12 months ahead
Sample		1998:01–2006:10			2004:01–2006:10	2004:01–2006:10		1998:01–2006:10
Number of observations		106			34	34		106
Source of inflationary expectations		consensus forecasts			Central Bank of Uruguay	Central Bank of Uruguay		consensus forecasts

Source: IMF staff estimates.

Notes for generalized method of moments estimates: Andrews bandwidth standard errors are given in parentheses. Instruments include inflation (–2), inflation (–3), primary balance/GDP (–3), real wage gap (–2), real wage gap (–3), money growth rate (–2), money growth rate (–3), DC, and DP. Estimates (5) and (6) exclude DC and DP as instruments, where DC and DP are dummy variables capturing two different effects of 2002 crisis. DC=1 in 2002:07–2003:2 period, thus it captures a transitory increase of inflationary expectations due to the crisis. DP=1 from 2003:3 onward, thereby it captures some structural changes after the crisis. The estimation results showed that only lagged inflation coefficients have experienced a structural change due to the 2002 crisis.

*, **, *** indicate significance at the 10, 5, and 1 percent level, respectively. — signifies a variable not included in the estimation.

Notes for cointegration equation estimates: standard errors are given in parentheses.

Figure 2.3. Determinants of Inflationary Expectations: Recursive Coefficients
(Recursive ordinary least squares (OLS) estimates on an annual horizon)

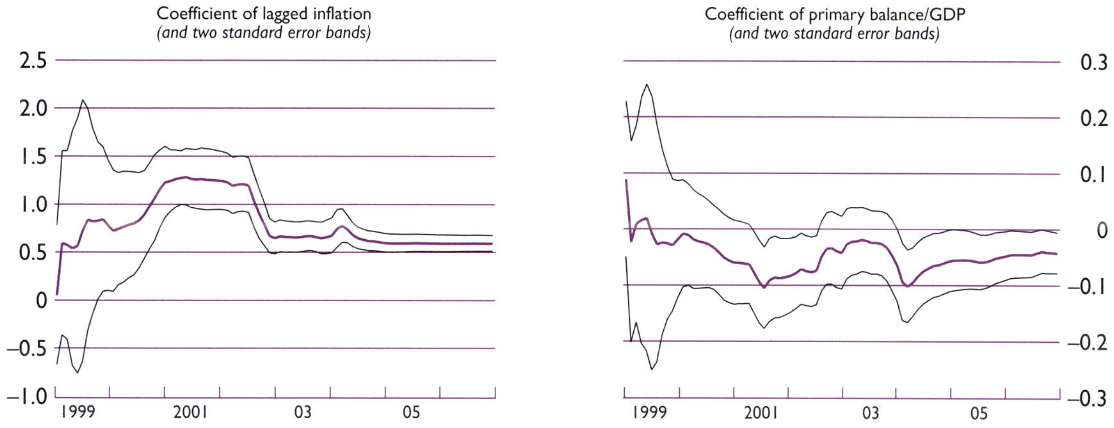

Source: IMF staff estimates.

where pb_{t-1} is the ratio of the consolidated primary fiscal balance to GDP, and the monetary variables include year-on-year M1 growth or, alternatively, exchange rate change (see Licandro and Vicente (2006) for a discussion of the link between fiscal policy and inflation objectives in Uruguay). It is also important to examine whether there has been a structural break in the postcrisis expectations formation using a dummy variable. Equation (2) is estimated by a GMM to address potential endogeneity problems, using both 12-month- and 1-month-ahead horizons.

The results suggest that lagged inflation, the primary balance, and marginal costs proxies explain expected inflation (Table 2.2). Monetary aggregates become important only after the adoption of a flexible exchange rate regime and do not play a role in shorter horizon forecasts. Changes in the nominal exchange rate affect expectations, but the effect is modest and not significant for one-month-ahead expectations. Lagged inflation contributes 50–60 percent to explaining expected inflation, although for one-month expectations, the contribution is significantly smaller. For the 12-month-ahead estimation, recursive coefficient estimates on lagged inflation stabilize around 0.6 after the adoption of a flexible exchange rate in 2002 (Figure 2.3).

The primary balance plays a role in determining expected inflation. It enters with a negative coefficient in almost all the estimated equations (see Celasun, Gelos, and Prati, 2004a and 2004b; and Cerisola and Gelos, forthcoming) and, for estimations with a 12-month-ahead horizon, the coefficient increased slightly since 2003. The quantitative significance of this factor is moderate, however: a 1 percent increase in the primary balance as a percentage of GDP is estimated to yield a fall in inflation expectations by about 0.5 percentage point. For a shorter forecast horizon, it is also significant but less important. The model tracks inflation expectations quite well, including during the crisis period (Figure 2.4).

There is some evidence that announced inflation targets have gained credibility. Inference is limited given that this study works with data starting January 2004, using the midpoint of the 12-month-ahead inflation target range. The coefficient on the inflation target is significant; on lagged inflation, it is insignificant. Recursive ordinary least squares (OLS) estimates show that the coefficient was approaching 1 during 2006 (Figure 2.5). These results suggest that forecasters are forward-looking and increasingly anchoring expectations around the central bank targets.[4] The notion of a recent increase in the central bank's credibility is consistent with the evolution of the dispersion of inflation forecasts. In particular, the coefficient of variation for survey expectations shows no clear trend until early 2006 and a decline since then (Figure 2.6). However, this result needs to be taken with caution. As discussed in the chapter by López-Mejía, Rebucci, and Saizar, before the switch to interest rate targeting in September 2007, there appeared to be some perceptions of ambiguity about the objectives and instruments of monetary policy that could have undermined monetary policy credibility.

[4]See Cerisola and Gelos (forthcoming) and Minella and others (2003) for similar results on the relevance of inflation targets for the case of Brazil.

Figure 2.4. Twelve-Month-Ahead Expected Inflation: Actual Versus Fitted (Generalized method of moments–based model)
(In percent)

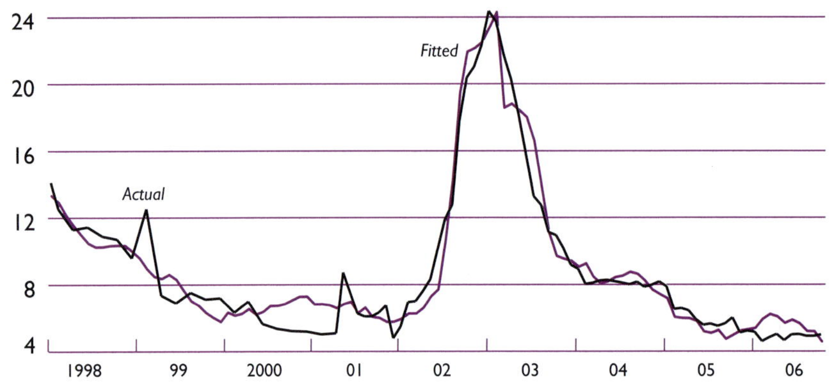

Source: Authors' calculations.

Figure 2.5. Recursive Estimates of Coefficient on Inflation Target (Recursive ordinary least squares estimates)
(Coefficient of inflation target and two standard error bands)

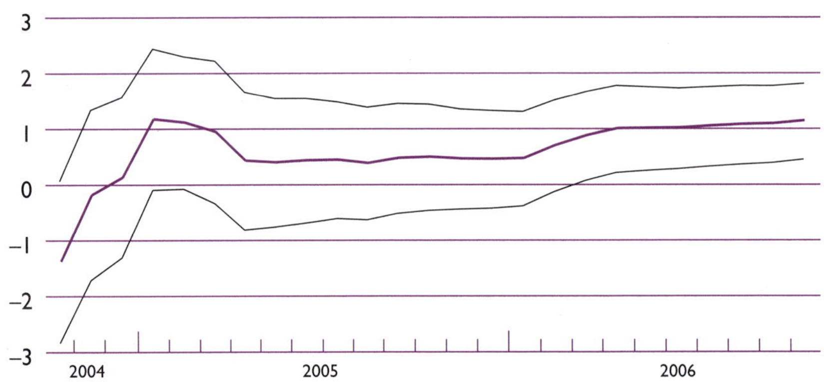

Source: IMF staff estimates.

Estimations taking into account possible nonstationarity reinforce the results. A Johansen cointegration test finds a stable relationship between expected inflation, lagged inflation, primary balance, real effective exchange rate, and real wage gap; a vector error correction (VEC) model suggests that the 12-month-ahead inflation forecasts are determined by lagged inflation, primary balance, and the marginal costs proxies. The estimated coefficients have the same signs and only slightly higher magnitudes than the GMM estimates.

Figure 2.6. Dispersion of Inflation Forecasts
(Coefficient of variation)

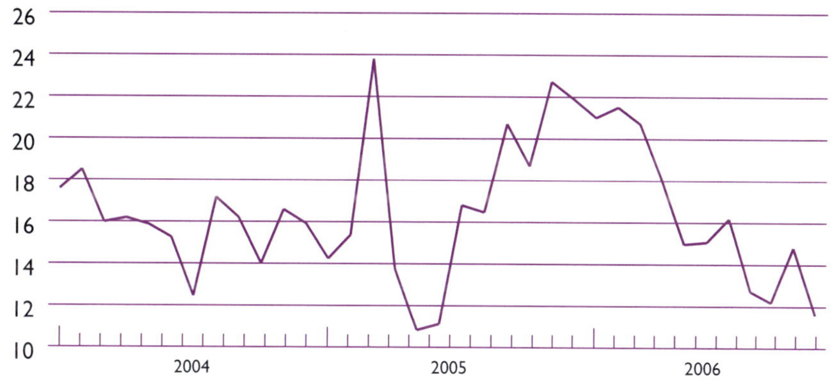

Source: IMF staff estimates.

Rationality

Are expectations rational? To explore this issue, this chapter first examines unbiasedness, regressing actual inflation on both an intercept and expected inflation:

$$\Pi_t = c + \beta\Pi_t^e + \varepsilon_t. \tag{3}$$

If expectations are unbiased, c should be zero and β one. This is the joint hypothesis tested in this chapter (Table 2.3).

The Central Bank of Uruguay inflation forecasts appear unbiased for 1 month ahead, but biased for 12 months ahead. However, the tests should be interpreted with caution given the potential nonstationarity of the series. Generally, the estimated coefficient of an $I(1)$ variable is not normally distributed, invalidating the usual tests. In any case, however, the paper would reject unbiasedness for the 12-month-ahead inflation expectations.[5,6]

Allowing for the possibility of nonstationarity, the results confirm that expectations do not use all available information. Johansen tests find a cointegration relation between actual and expected inflation (Appendix Table 2A.1). The speed at which expectations are revised over time in light of new information is estimated through a bivariate VEC model with inflation and expected inflation (Appendix Table 2A.2). If the parameter on the expectation error in this regression is significant, then consumers revise their expectations and adjust them toward the fully rational outcome. The estimated coefficients are negative and significant for both the 12-month-ahead and 1-month-ahead forecasts, implying low persistence in deviation between actual and expected inflation. However, regressions of the forecast errors on different variables indicate that 12-month-ahead forecasts fail to extract all possible information from all the relevant variables,[7] except for past information on the real effective exchange rate gap. On the other hand, one-month-ahead forecasts seem efficient in the use of past information, except for the informational content of actual inflation (Appendix Table 2A.3).

Conclusions

This chapter examined the role of inflation expectations in shaping inflation dynamics, the degree of inflation persistence, and the rationality and factors driving inflation expectations. The key results are as follows:

- Inflation expectations are more important than past inflation in shaping the inflation process. As a result, inflation inertia is not high. However, recent changes in wage agreement mechanisms containing backward-looking elements may lead to an increase in inertia. In the most recent wage

[5]See similar results for other Latin American countries in de Carvalho and Bugarin (2006).

[6]The results are not an artifact from the approximation for the 12-month forecasts because unbiasedness is also rejected for much shorter subperiods.

[7]This result also holds for the shorter 12-month survey available from the central bank.

Table 2.3. Tests of Unbiasedness of Inflation Forecasts

Coefficients	Consensus Forecasts	Central Bank of Uruguay
α	–0.031	–0.004
β	1.35	1.46
Adjusted R^2	0.89	0.382948
Coefficient (p-values)	consensus forecasts	Central Bank of Uruguay
$\alpha = 0$	0.0001	0.052
$\beta = 1$	0.0001	0.0816
$\alpha = 0$ and $\beta = 1$	0.0003	0.1265
Sample period	1998:01–2006:09	2004:01–2006:09

Source: IMF staff estimates.

negotiations, emphasis has been shifted again to forward-looking adjustments.

- Moreover, the role of lagged inflation in shaping the inflation process has been declining since 2002.
- Confirming previous studies' results, fiscal variables play a role in driving inflation expectations, with a higher primary balance associated with lower expected inflation.
- The evidence suggests that the central bank has gained credibility since the adoption of a flexible exchange rate and the announcement of inflation targets. Forecasters increasingly take the central bank's targets into account when forming expectations.
- Twelve-month-ahead inflation expectations are neither unbiased nor efficient, whereas one-month-ahead inflation surveys are.

For policy purposes, low inertia implies that responding to inflationary shocks entails more limited output losses. The results also underscore the role of consistent macroeconomic policies for anchoring inflation expectations, with fiscal credibility playing an important role. The increase in credibility of the central bank since the move to a flexible exchange rate regime bodes well for a gradual move to a full-fledged inflation-targeting regime. As discussed in the next chapter, further increasing credibility will require increasing the clarity of objectives and procedures of monetary policy. Still, the evidence on the rationality of the forecasts is mixed. This suggests that further efforts at enhancing policy communications may help agents improve their forecasts and assist the authorities in anchoring expectations.

Appendix 2.1. Cointegration Tests, Bivariate Vector Error Correction Model, and Tests of Efficiency of Inflation Forecasts

Table 2A.1. Johansen Cointegration Test Results

	Trace Statistic for Alternative Trend Assumptions: Source of Inflationary Expectations	
	Consensus forecasts	Central Bank of Uruguay
No intercept, no trend	12.7 (0.043)	35.3 (0.00)
An intercept, no trend	20.3 (0.049)	49.6 (0.00)
An intercept, a linear trend	19.9 (0.01)	49.1 (0.00)
An intercept and a trend, a linear trend	29.3 (0.018)	52.3 (0)
An intercept, quadratic trend	29.3 (0.001)	51.5 (0)

Source: IMF staff estimates.

p–values for the null: none; cointegrating equations are reported in parentheses. Two lags were used as indicated by Schwartz criterion.

Table 2A.2. Adjustment Coefficients in a Bivariate Vector Error Correction on Actual and Expected Inflation

Source of Inflationary Expectations	Consensus Forecasts, 12 Months Ahead	
	Expectations regression	Actual inflation regression
Adjustment coefficients	–0.15*	0.13*
t-statistics	–0.067	–0.061
Sample period	1998:01–2006:09	
	Central Bank of Uruguay, 1 Month Ahead	
	Expectations regression	Actual inflation regression
Adjustment coefficients	–1.41*	–0.63
t-statistics	–0.34	–1.05
Sample period	2004:04–2006:09	

Source: IMF staff estimates.

Table 2A.3. Tests of Efficiency of Inflation Forecasts

12-month-ahead forecast horizon
Sample period: 1993:03–2006:09
Number of observations: 163

Dependent variable	Regressors	Chi-square	p-value
ε_{t+12}	Constant, lags 1 to 3 of inflation	21.71	0.0002
ε_{t+12}	Constant, lags 1 to 3 of primary balance	10.42	0.034
ε_{t+12}	Constant, lags 1 to 3 of real wage gap	19.24084	0.0007
ε_{t+12}	Constant, lags 1 to 3 of real effective exchange rate gap	8.933186	0.0628
ε_{t+12}	Constant, lags 1 to 3 of year-on-year M1 growth	18.59057	0.0009
ε_{t+12}	Constant, lags 1 to 3 of unemployment rate	25.35912	0.00
ε_{t+12}	Constant, lags 1 to 3 of year-on-year exchange rate change	70.51959	0.00

1-month-ahead forecast horizon
Sample period: 2004:01–2006:09
Number of observations: 33

Dependent variable	Regressors	Chi-square	p-value
ε_{t+1}	Constant, lags 1 to 3 of inflation	14.60901	0.0056
ε_{t+1}	Constant, lags 1 to 3 of primary balance	5.496805***	0.24
ε_{t+1}	Constant, lags 1 to 3 of real wage gap	2.534467	0.6385
ε_{t+1}	Constant, lags 1 to 3 of real effective exchange rate gap	9.135744	0.0578
ε_{t+1}	Constant, lags 1 to 3 of year-on-year M1 growth	4.018122	0.4036
ε_{t+1}	Constant, lags 1 to 3 of unemployment rate	2.907312	0.5735
ε_{t+1}	Constant, lags 1 to 3 of year-on-year exchange rate change	6.910537	0.1407

Source: IMF staff estimates.
*** indicates significance at the 1 percent level.

Bibliography

Beeby, Mark, Stephan Hall, and Brian Henry, 2001, "Rational Expectations and Near Rational Alternatives: How Best to Form Expectations," ECB Working Paper No. 86 (Brussels: European Central Bank).

Barkbu, Bergljot, and Nicoletta Batini, 2005, "The New Keynesian Phillips Curve When Inflation Is Non-Stationary: The Case for Canada," paper presented at Bank of Canada conference, "Issues in Inflation Targeting," Ottawa, April 28–29.

Batini, Nicoletta, 2006, "Inflation Persistence in Latin America?" paper prepared for the Latin American and Caribbean Economic Association meeting, Mexico City, November 2.

Celasun, Oya, R. Gaston Gelos, and Alessandro Prati, 2004a, "Would 'Cold Turkey' Work in Turkey?" *IMF Staff Papers*, Vol. 51 (November), pp. 493–509.

———, 2004b, "Obstacles to Disinflation: What Is the Role of Fiscal Expectations?" *Economic Policy*, Vol. 19 (October), pp. 441–81.

Celasun, Oya, and Donal McGettigan, 2005, "Turkey's Inflation Process," in *Turkey at the Crossroads—From Crisis Resolution to EU Accession*, IMF Occasional Paper No. 242 (Washington: International Monetary Fund).

Cerisola, Martin, and Gaston Gelos, forthcoming, "What Drives Inflation Expectations in Brazil? An Empirical Analysis," *Applied Economics*.

Clemente, J., A. Montañés, and M. Reyes, 1998, "Testing for Unit Root in Variables with a Double Change in the Mean," *Economics Letters*, Vol. 59 (May), pp. 175–82.

Consensus Economics (various issues).

de Carvalho, Fabia, and Maurício Bugarin, 2006, "Inflation Expectations in Latin America," *Economia*, Vol. 6 (Spring), pp. 101–45.

Fildes, Robert, and Herman Stekler, 2002, "The State of Macroeconomic Forecasting," *Journal of Macroeconomics*, Vol. 24 (December), pp. 435–68.

Forsells, Magnus, and Geoff Kenny, 2002, "The Rationality of Consumers' Inflation Expectations: Survey-based Evidence for the Euro Area," ECB Working Paper No. 163 (Brussels: European Central Bank).

Galí, Jordi, and Mark Gertler, 1999, "Inflation Dynamics: A Structural Econometric Analysis," *Journal of Monetary Economics*, Vol. 44 (October), pp. 195–222.

Gertler, Mark, 2004, "Discussion of Structural Inflation Modeling Papers," paper presented at a conference on "Inflation Persistence in the Euro Area," European Central Bank, Frankfurt am Main, Germany, December 10–11. Available via the Internet: www.ecb.int/events/pdf/conferences/inflationpersistence/Gertlersession5.pdf.

Johansen, Soren, and Anders Rygh Swensen, 1999, "Testing Some Exact Rational Expectations in Vectors Autoregressive Models," *Journal of Econometrics*, Vol. 93, pp. 73–91.

Licandro, Gerardo, and Leonardo Vicente, 2006, "Incentivos Fiscales e Inconsistencia Temporal: Uruguay 1970–2005" (unpublished; Montevideo: Central Bank of Uruguay).

Minella, A., P. Springer de Freitas, I. Goldfajn, and M.K. Muinhos, 2003, "Inflation Targeting in Brazil: Constructing Credibility under Exchange Rate Volatility," *Journal of International Money and Finance*, Vol. 22 (December), pp. 1015–40.

Paquet, Alain, 1992, "Inflationary Expectations and Rationality," *Economics Letters*, Vol. 40 (November), pp. 303–08.

Roberts, J.M., 1995, "New Keynesian Economics and the Phillips Curve," *Journal of Money, Credit and Banking*, Vol. 27 (November), pp. 975–84.

———, 1997, "Is Inflation Sticky?" *Journal of Monetary Economics*, Vol. 39 (July), pp. 173–96.

III Pass-Through, Dollarization, and Credibility in Uruguay

Alejandro López-Mejía, Alessandro Rebucci, and Carolina Saizar

A high degree of exchange rate pass-through to domestic prices and financial dollarization can constrain the effectiveness of a flexible exchange rate as a shock absorber and indirect channel of transmission of monetary policy. Accordingly, pass-through and financial dollarization have been considered key obstacles to the design and implementation of an independent monetary policy in Uruguay since the 2002 crisis, when the exchange rate was allowed to float. A poorly (well-) functioning monetary policy framework in a flexible exchange rate regime, in turn, may hamper (foster) the country's ability to maintain macroeconomic stability and insulate the real side of the economy from shocks.

This chapter documents the recent evolution of pass-through and investigates the scope for reducing dollarization through enhanced monetary policy credibility. In line with developments in other emerging markets, this chapter finds that exchange rate pass-through in Uruguay has declined over the years. However, the results suggest that it has become volatile and unstable since late 2005, when the authorities moved away from the free float adopted in the aftermath of the 2002 crisis. Also, consistent with theory and other experiences (see Jeanne, 2003; Borensztein and others, 2004; and Rajan, 2004, among others), it finds that monetary policy credibility affects financial dollarization, although long periods of time may be needed for credibility to deliver its benefits and for dollarization to decline.

The policy implications of these findings are important. A lower exchange rate pass-through to domestic prices implies that the exchange rate can work well as a shock absorber and is less effective as a nominal anchor. Thus, the exchange rate could be allowed to float more freely in response to normal shocks. To the extent that positive capital account shocks have a temporary component, greater exchange rate flexibility would be consistent with "leaning against the wind" to accumulate reserves further, thus adding insurance against balance of payments crises. Given that, with high dollarization, large exchange rate fluctuations generate balance sheet effects that can destabilize the real economy and the financial sector,[1] greater flexibility is also consistent with intervening for foreign exchange liquidity provisions in response to sudden and large negative capital account shocks. Improving credibility should become a priority because it can help lower dollarization, reducing vulnerabilities to external shocks and enhancing the transmission mechanisms of monetary policy. This, in turn, would increase the economy's ability to implement effective stabilization policies, thus fostering an environment conducive to financial development and growth.

Background

This section describes the evolution of the monetary policy framework and the constraints to the channels of transmission of monetary policy in Uruguay. It underlines the importance of increasing the clarity of objectives and the transparency of operations under the existing framework to increase credibility.

Evolution of the Monetary Policy Framework

Uruguay's long history of monetary instability came to an end with a successful exchange-rate-based stabilization during the 1990s. Starting in late 1990, the authorities allowed the peso to move within a crawling band that was depreciated at a declining rate, but in excess of domestic inflation, to help strengthen external competitiveness. This policy helped anchor inflationary expectations and brought inflation down to 4 percent in 1999 from more than 100 percent in 1990 (Figure 3.1).

A revealed preference for single-digit inflation has emerged since the late 1990s. During the past eight years, average annual inflation has fluctuated within 3½ and 9⅓ percent. An exception was 2002, when end-year inflation reached 26 percent following the financial crisis—still a moderate increase compared with the inflation experienced in previous decades.[2]

[1]These implications are consistent with a formal analysis of alternative monetary policy responses in economies potentially vulnerable to sudden stops (Benigno and others, 2007 and forthcoming).

[2]The crisis was triggered by deposit withdrawals from cash-strapped Argentine residents that soon developed into a more generalized run on the banks (IMF, 2003).

Figure 3.1. Inflation in Uruguay
(Twelve-month rate)

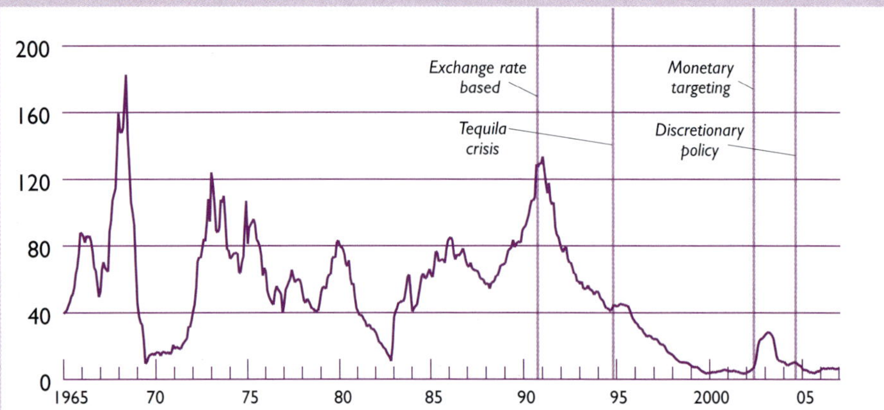

Source: Central Bank of Uruguay.

The monetary framework that was adopted in the midst of the 2002 financial crisis has evolved gradually. Initially, the exchange rate was allowed to float in June 2002, and base money targets were selected to anchor the system starting in early 2003. In 2004, a band for base money (rather than a point) became the monetary target and, at the end of each quarter, the central bank began to announce a target for the annual headline consumer price inflation 12 months in advance. In late 2005, the authorities moved away from the free float and adopted M1 as the intermediate target, keeping the base money range as the operational target; since then, significant foreign exchange purchases, partly undertaken by the government to meet its foreign currency needs, have succeeded in maintaining the nominal exchange rate as broadly stable (Figure 3.2). In 2006, the central bank stopped announcing base money targets and extended the inflation target band to 18 months (still with the possibility of revising it at the end of each quarter) (de Brun and Licandro, 2006; and Aboal, Lanzilotta, and Perera, 2006) and, in September 2007, it announced a switch from indicative M1 targets to interest rate targeting.

Under these circumstances, and particularly before the switch to interest rate targeting, the monetary framework appeared to have multiple objectives. Indeed, by mid-2007, the authorities appeared to be simultaneously targeting (and announcing) M1 and the inflation rate, and they had an apparent exchange rate target. This ambiguity could also reflect the fact that the mandate of the central bank is not exclusively to maintain low inflation. According to the law, other objectives of the central bank are to maintain an adequate level of international reserves and the stability of the financial system. In addition, although an exchange rate objective is not specified in the central bank's formal mandate, the exchange rate has in practice been a policy objective because of concerns related to competitiveness and the balance sheet effects associated with dollarization.

Consistency among the main objectives of monetary policy is essential. Whereas the exchange rate was a clear and transparent nominal anchor during the 1990s, the appearance of multiple objectives and insufficient clarity on the relative importance of each of these objectives under the monetary framework could leave the system without a clear anchor and undermine its credibility. For instance, if the exchange rate is perceived as a policy objective per se, the authorities' inflation target may be ignored by the public when forming their expectations about inflation. Thus, there is a strong need to be transparent regarding the role of the exchange rate to help strengthen the effectiveness of monetary policy (Mishkin and Savastano, 2000). In this context, limiting foreign exchange intervention by the state bank would minimize market perceptions of exchange rate "floors" and needs to be coordinated with the central bank (Aboal, Lorenzo, and Noya, 2003). Steps in the right direction were taken in the second half of 2007: the peso was allowed to appreciate by about 9 percent against the dollar, and direct intervention by the government was limited.

Figure 3.2. Nominal Exchange Rate and Foreign Exchange Rate Intervention

(Foreign exchange purchase in millions of U.S. dollars)

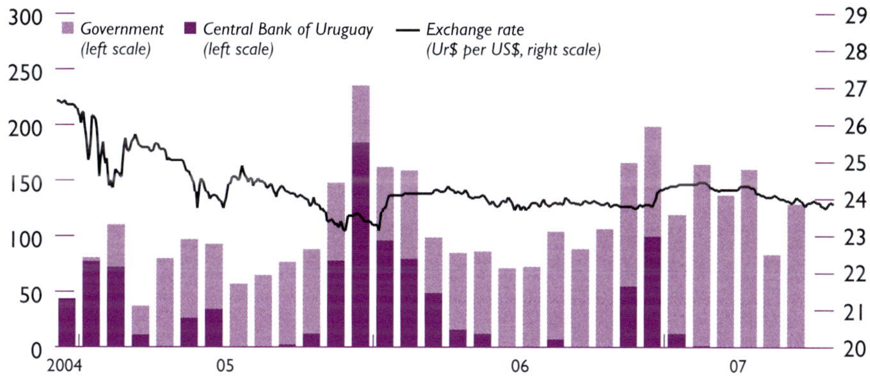

Source: Central Bank of Uruguay.

Transmission Mechanisms of Monetary Policy and Their Implications

The channels through which monetary policy is transmitted to prices and output face several constraints in Uruguay. If the exchange rate plays a key role in the price-setting process, a flexible exchange rate could lead to high variability in inflation and increase dollarization (Ize and Levy Yeyati, 2006). A high pass-through also reduces the effectiveness of the exchange rate as an indirect channel of transmission to output and prices because changes in the exchange rate would have a limited impact on net exports. The existence of a high pass-through in Uruguay is consistent with a large share of tradable goods in the consumer basket (about 60 percent).[3] Also, a history of monetary instability might have led the public to try to isolate the impact of changes in the exchange rate on real income by linking price and wage contracts to changes in the value of the peso against the dollar.

High financial dollarization makes inflation expectations harder to anchor and reduces the effectiveness of monetary policy to affect aggregate demand. High financial dollarization reduces the effectiveness of the interest rate channel because the central bank has limited control over the dollar yield curve of interest rates. Thus, changes in money supply in domestic currency have a limited impact on savings and aggregate demand (see Varela-Loschiavo and Vera Iglesias, 2003). Dollarization also weakens the exchange rate channel: an expansionary monetary policy, which could increase the demand for domestic goods through the impact of a real devaluation, may lead to financial distress and an economic contraction owing to balance sheet effects.

Low financial intermediation and the structure of the financial system also weaken the channels of monetary policy transmission. With relatively low financial intermediation, personal savings and retained earnings play a key role in financing consumption and investment, and the effectiveness of the interest rate and lending channels is more limited (Figure 3.3).[4] Also, in the case of Uruguay, the presence of a large state-owned bank, representing about 50 percent of the system, potentially weakens the lending channel. A monetary contraction, for example, may not necessarily lead to a reduction of the bank's loanable resources because the government can have an incentive to provide the bank with the needed resources to avoid a reduction in lending and output. Still, as discussed by Gelos and Piñón in Chapter IV, the lending channel, although still low, is becoming more important.

Enhancing the credibility of monetary policy would help relax these constraints. Credibility is essential

[3]A high pass-through is usually associated with high real dollarization (Armas, Batini, and Tuesta, 2007). In Uruguay, available evidence indicates that the elasticity of prices with respect to the exchange rate is about 0.5 in the long run (Licandro, 2000).

[4]De Brun and others (2008) find that retained earnings and bank lending represent 45 and 25 percent of total financing of corporations, respectively.

Figure 3.3. A Measure of Financial Sector Development
(M2 in percent of GDP, 12-month moving average)

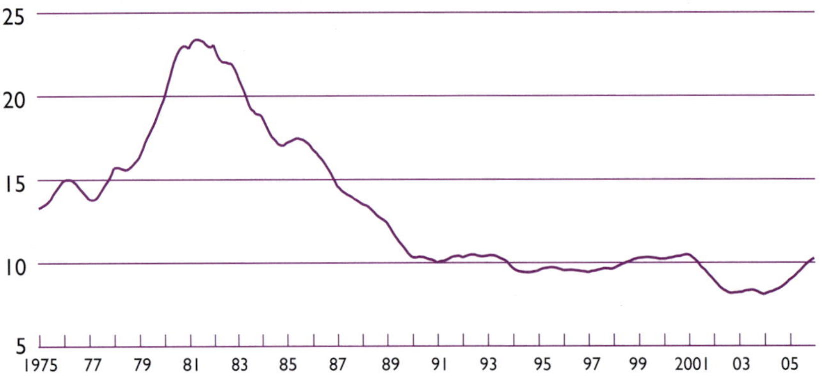

Source: Central Bank of Uruguay.

for the expectation channel of monetary policy to work and for a sustained process of dedollarization to occur. Reduced dollarization would help increase the effectiveness of other transmission channels and makes monetary policy more effective in stabilizing the economy. This, in turn, could lead the private sector to require less real and financial hedging against the risk of instability, thus reducing dollarization and the vulnerability of the economy to crisis. The next two sections study the evolution of pass-through and investigate the scope for reducing financial dollarization through enhanced credibility.

Has Pass-Through Declined in Uruguay?

A standard methodology was used to assess the evolution of the exchange rate pass-through to the consumer price index (CPI) and the producer price index (PPI). Following Campa and Goldberg (2002), as adapted by Edwards (2006) to the analysis of changes in exchange rate pass-through after the adoption of inflation-targeting regimes, we estimated the following equation by ordinary least squares using monthly data:

$$\Delta \log P_t = \beta_0 + \beta_1 \Delta \log E_t + \beta_3 \Delta \log P_t^* + \beta_4 \Delta \log P_{t-1} + \omega_t, \qquad (1)$$

where P_t is the price index (the CPI and PPI were used as proxies for nontradables and tradables inflation, respectively), E_t is the nominal exchange rate, P_t^* is the U.S. PPI (a proxy for world inflation), and ω_t is an error term with standard characteristics. The short-term pass-through is given by β_1, and the long-term pass-through is $\beta_1/(1-\beta_4)$. For a nominal exchange rate to be an effective shock absorber or help transmit monetary policy impulses indirectly, the pass-through for nontradables needs to be smaller than that for tradables: a nominal devaluation leads to a real depreciation, helping generate an expenditure switching effect, thus affecting net exports and the output gap.

The results indicate that the pass-through has declined since the 2002 crisis, and it is now higher for tradables than for nontradables. Table 3.1 presents the estimated short-run and long-run pass-through coefficients for the CPI and PPI equations for Uruguay and a set of comparator countries analyzed by Edwards (2006). In the case of Uruguay, the sample is divided into precrisis (September 1990–September 2002) and postcrisis (December 2002–September 2005) periods. The pass-through coefficient (short and long term) declined after the 2002 crisis for tradable and nontradable goods. Although the pass-through coefficients for nontradables are now lower than for tradables, they were higher before the 2002 crisis—probably because of the importance of backward-looking wage indexation mechanisms during the 1990s. The pass-through coefficients vary considerably across countries, with higher values in economies that experienced high inflation (e.g., Brazil, Israel, Mexico, and Uruguay).

An alternative methodology yields similar insights. Static ordinary least squares rolling regressions with different estimation windows, each of which can be

Table 3.1. Short- and Long-Run Exchange Rate Pass-Through, Selected Countries

	Consumer Price Index				Producer Price Index			
	Short-run pass-through		Long-run pass-through		Short-run pass-through		Long-run pass-through	
Country	Pre–inflation targeting	Post–inflation targeting	Pre–inflation targeting	Post–inflation targeting	Pre–inflation targeting	Post–inflation targeting	Pre–inflation targeting	Post–inflation targeting
Uruguay[1]	0.56	0.24	1.4	0.45	0.41	0.39	1.17	0.76
Australia	0.054	0.000	0.120	0.000	0.070	0.070	0.070	0.070
Brazil	0.719	0.056	1.027	. . .	0.759	0.235	1.060	0.697
Canada	0.039	0.000	0.078	0.000	0.085	0.085	0.143	0.143
Chile	0.137	0.005	0.212	0.008	0.207	0.045	0.257	0.056
Israel	0.624	0.197	0.718	. . .	0.627	0.197	0.713	0.224
Korea	0.020	0.020	0.025	0.025	0.055	0.055	0.070	0.070
Mexico	0.191	0.015	0.523	0.018	0.246	0.246	0.591	0.316

Source: Edwards (2007).

[1]Before and after the 2002 crisis; monthly data. The specification includes one lag (or automatic specification search starting from six lags in Pcgets) before the crisis. After the crisis, automatic specification search is used, starting from six lags.

Figure 3.4. Pass-Through Rolling Regression Coefficients

Source: IMF staff estimates.

interpreted as a cointegration relation, indicate that the pass-through to the CPI began to decline much earlier (around 1994–95) as the level and volatility of inflation declined (Figure 3.4). Although the regressions suggest a sharp increase in the pass-through following the 2002 crisis, they also show a subsequent decline to below the precrisis level, consistent with the results in Table 3.1. However, the switch to a managed float regime seems to be associated with a strong instability of the pass-through, with the 12-month window suggesting that it could be on the rise again.

The exchange rate cannot be an effective nominal anchor when the pass-through is unstable. Indeed, under these circumstances, exchange rate movements have an uncertain impact on inflation. At the same time, the exchange rate is now a more effective shock absorber, with the exchange rate pass-through for nontradables being smaller than that for tradables. Therefore, the exchange rate should be allowed to float more freely in response to normal shocks. Nevertheless, high dollarization is still a constraint to a floating exchange rate because large fluctuations would induce destabilizing balance sheet effects.

Is Monetary Policy Credibility Linked to Financial Dollarization?

Financial dollarization is very high and persistent in Uruguay. A traditional measure of financial dollarization is the share of dollar deposits in total deposits of the banking system (Figure 3.5). Financial dollarization can also be measured as the share of dollar credit in total credit of the banking system (Figure 3.6). In Uruguay, both measures of dollarization are very high and persistent, with credit dollarization somewhat lower and more volatile than deposit dollarization.

Credibility can be broadly defined as the public's degree of confidence or uncertainty regarding the government's policy objectives. Monetary policy credibility can thus be measured as the probabilistic distance between the expected policy outturns and the publicly announced policy targets. The measure adopted here is

Figure 3.5. Deposit Dollarization
(Dollar deposits, in percent of total deposits)

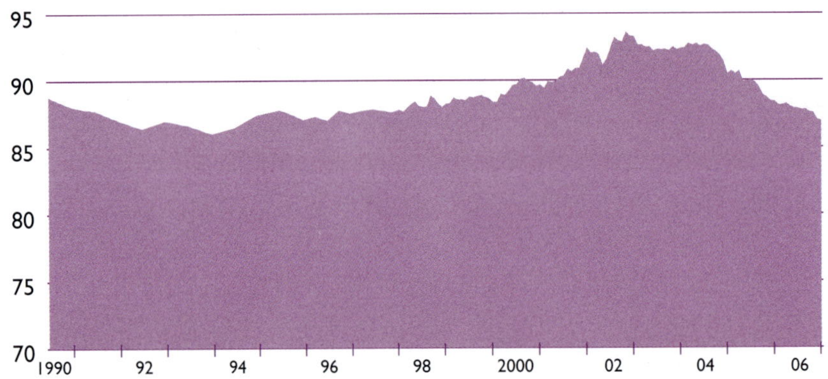

Source: Central Bank of Uruguay.

Figure 3.6. Credit Dollarization
(Dollar lending, in percent of total lending)

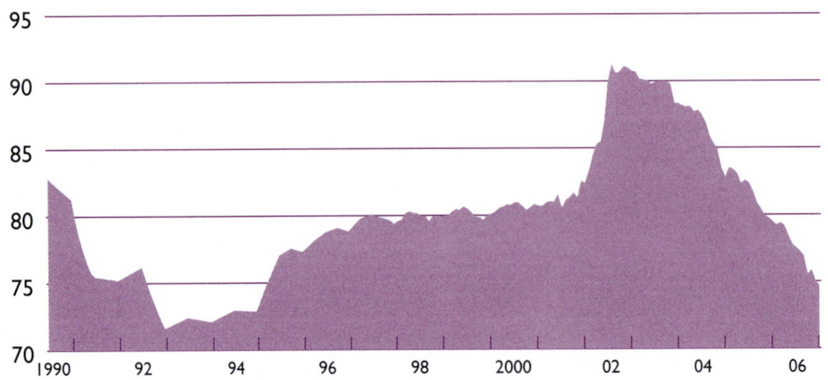

Source: Central Bank of Uruguay.

Figure 3.7. A Measure of Credibility
(Index[1])

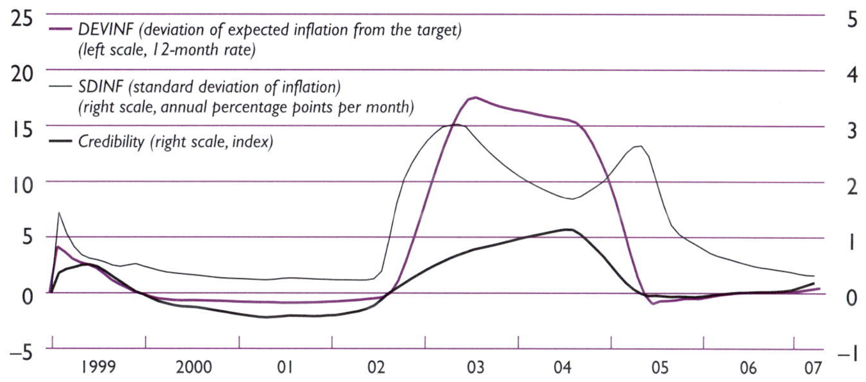

Source: IMF staff estimates.
[1]See main text for description.

the difference between expected inflation and the inflation target, normalized by the variance of expected inflation. Thus, credibility = $(E\pi_t - T\pi_t)/(8^*V\pi_t$^0.5), where $E\pi_t$ is expected (unconditional) mean inflation at time t, $T\pi_t$ is the inflation target, and $V\pi_t$^0.5 is the standard deviation of unconditional mean inflation. This measure is approximately bounded between –1 and +1, if the standard deviation of mean inflation is multiplied by a factor of 8, and theoretically "perfect" when expected inflation is equal to the inflation target at zero.[5] The numerator quantifies the distance between expected inflation and the inflation target (that is, it provides a signal on the direction and magnitude of the deviation of expectations from target). The denominator quantifies the uncertainty regarding such deviations (the noise surrounding the signal). For instance, a large deviation of expectations from the inflation target associated with high uncertainty may result in the same credibility level as a relatively smaller deviation with lower uncertainty.

According to this measure, credibility has fluctuated widely since the late 1990s and has lately declined. Broadly in line with previous findings (Masoller, 1997), monetary policy credibility appears to have been very "close to perfect" during the last years of the exchange-rate-based stabilization period, reflecting a small undershooting of expected inflation compared with the target and little uncertainty about those deviations.[6] Credibility started to deteriorate just before the crisis, but it took three years before reverting to the precrisis levels. This latter improvement was partly the result of a second wave of uncertainty, possibly associated with the changes in the monetary procedures and framework in 2005 (Figure 3.7). However, according to this measure of credibility, between 2006 and mid-2007 there was a moderate deterioration in credibility, with small deviations of expected inflation from the target associated with progressively less uncertainty about those deviations.

Financial dollarization and credibility are closely associated. This holds for the pre- and postcrisis periods, with a sample correlation of around 0.8, and is confirmed by a more formal analysis (Figure 3.8). A simple vector autoregression (VAR) analysis shows that lower credibility increases dollarization persistently (Figure 3.9).[7] Thus, enhancing the credibility of monetary policy could help reduce financial dollarization, which, in turn, would make monetary policy more effective. However, consistent with evidence from other countries (Borensztein and others, 2004), it is likely to take a long time for credibility to deliver its benefits and for dollarization to decline. For instance, between Feb-

[5]See Appendix 3.1 for more details.

[6]This evidence is robust to two alternative measures of credibility: the difference between consensus forecast inflation and the inflation targets under the IMF programs, and the difference between expected depreciation (as implied by the interest rate differential between dollar and peso bank deposits) and actual depreciation under the upper band of the crawl.

[7]For identification purposes, the VAR assumes that dollarization does not affect credibility within a month. The VAR includes the measure of credibility and the share of dollar deposits in total deposits by residents, together with three lags of each variable, a constant and a linear trend, and Argentine and Uruguayan country spreads. Data are monthly, and the sample period is from January 1999 to December 2006.

Figure 3.8. Financial Dollarization and Credibility

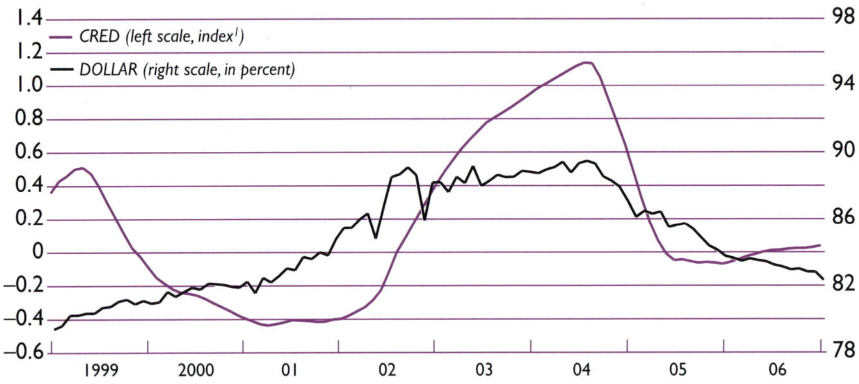

Source: IMF staff estimates.
[1]See main text for description.

ruary 2004 and May 2005, credibility improved from one to zero, but deposit dollarization changed by only 4 percentage points (to 90 percent of total deposits).

Conclusions

The exchange rate pass-through to domestic prices has declined over the past decade, although it has become unstable since late 2005. This implies that the exchange rate is now a less effective nominal anchor; therefore, the role of an appreciation in offsetting inflationary pressures, although still important, has diminished. It also means that the exchange rate can generate expenditure-switching effects, thus helping isolate the economy from shocks. Accordingly, the exchange rate should be allowed to float more freely in response to normal shocks. However, high dollarization is still a

Figure 3.9. Impulse Response Functions

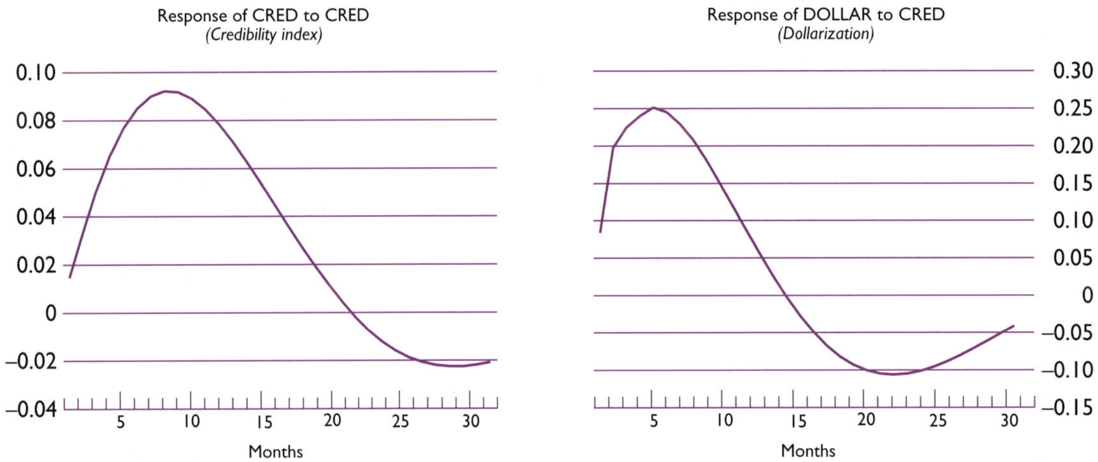

Source: IMF staff estimates.

constraint to a floating exchange rate because exchange rate fluctuations generate balance sheet effects that can destabilize the real economy and the financial sector. In this context, intervening in the foreign exchange market in response to financial shocks is justifiable. Clarity of the rationale for intervening and transparency of intervention procedures may help increase the effectiveness of such interventions and facilitate floating more freely in response to other shocks.

Improving monetary policy credibility would help reduce dollarization, a key constraint to monetary policy in Uruguay. Enhancing credibility would strengthen the expectation channel of monetary policy and, by reducing dollarization, would increase the effectiveness of other transmission channels and make monetary policy more credible for stabilizing the economy. This, in turn, could lead the private sector to require less hedging against the risk of instability, thus reducing the vulnerability of the economy to crisis and increasing long-term growth prospects.

There is scope to secure credibility gains in Uruguay. In particular, the credibility of its monetary framework can be improved by (1) strengthening de facto the operational independence of the central bank through its recapitalization and a clear commitment to subordinating the exchange rate to the inflation target, (2) enhancing the communication strategy to ensure that markets understand well the monetary policy strategy and the instruments and procedures for its implementation, (3) further strengthening the financial sector to help increase the effectiveness of monetary policy, and (4) further developing analytical capabilities to enhance the capacity of the central bank to forecast inflation and to understand better how adjustments in policy settings are transmitted into inflation.

Appendix 3.1. Measuring Credibility

The methodology adopted to measure credibility is that proposed by Rebucci and Rossi (2006; the RATS code is available on request from the authors). The procedure assumes that a representative agent "learns" in a Bayesian manner, knowing the econometric model of the inflation process, but with only beliefs (that is, prior probability distributions) about its parameters. The agent updates these beliefs on the basis of realizations of the inflation process to form posterior distributions about inflation and its characteristics. By manipulating these posterior distributions, a statistical or probabilistic measure of the distance between actual and target inflation, after each realization of the inflation process, can be computed.

To implement this methodology, three objects are needed: first, an inflation target; second, an econometric model of the disinflation process; and third, an estimation procedure to implement econometrically Bayesian learning about the inflation process and its characteristics. The assumed inflation target is a single-digit inflation range, between 4 and 6 percent, similar to the current inflation target of the authorities; alternative values for the target—namely, 4, 5, or 6 percent—yield similar results (not reported). It was assumed that inflation follows a simple autoregressive of degree one (AR1) process: $\pi_t = \alpha + \beta\pi_{t-1} + e_t$; $e_t \sim N(0, \sigma^2)$, where α is the conditional mean of inflation, β is the conditional persistence of temporary deviations from this mean, and σ^2 is the conditional volatility of the shocks producing these deviations.

The procedure focuses on the unconditional mean of inflation, given by $\alpha/(1-\beta)$. The mixed estimator is used to update the posterior distributions of α and β after each realization of the inflation process, thus providing for a very simple estimation procedure (see Rebucci and Rossi, 2006). For instance, given agents' prior on the model parameters at time $T-1$, say $\alpha(T-1)$ and $\beta(T-1)$, where $T-1$ is the month before the inflation target announcement, mixed estimation of the equation above over the sample period from $T-S$ to T, where S is the fixed length of the estimation window (24 months in our application), provides a posterior distribution of $\alpha(T)$ and $\beta(T)$. These posterior distributions can then be used as prior for $T+1$, and the posterior at time $T+1$ as prior at $T+2$, and so on. Given a sequence of posterior distributions, which are approximately normal if computed based on mixed estimation of the inflation equation above, the approximate expected value and standard deviation of $(\alpha/(1-\beta))$ can be easily computed, and hence our credibility measure described in the main text. Specifically, it can be shown that, for a given joint distribution of (α, β), the mean and the standard deviation of $g(\alpha,\beta) = (\alpha/(1-\beta))$ can be approximated as follows:

$$E[g(\alpha,\beta)] \approx g(E\alpha,E\beta) + 0.5 \cdot V[\alpha] \cdot \partial^2 g(E\alpha,E\beta)/\partial\alpha^2 + 0.5 \cdot V[\beta]\partial^2 g(E\alpha,E\beta)/\partial\beta^2 + \mathrm{Cov}[\alpha,\beta] \cdot \partial^2 g(E\alpha,E\beta)/\partial\alpha\partial\beta,$$

$$\mathrm{Var}[(\alpha,\beta)] \approx V[\alpha] \cdot \{\partial g(E\alpha,E\beta)/\partial\alpha\}2 + V[\beta] \cdot \{\partial g(E\alpha,E\beta)/\partial\beta\}2 + 2\mathrm{Cov}[\alpha,\beta] \cdot \{\partial g(E\alpha,E\beta)/\partial\alpha \cdot \partial g(E\alpha,E\beta)/\partial\beta\},$$

where $E\alpha$, $E\beta$, $V[\alpha]$, $V[\beta]$, and $\mathrm{Cov}[\alpha,\beta]$ are the moments of the joint distribution of (α,β).

Bibliography

Aboal, D., B. Lanzilotta, and M. Perera, 2006, "Flotación *de jure y de facto*?: La Política Monetaria-Cambiaria en el Período Pos Crisis en Uruguay" (unpublished; Montevideo: Centro de Investigaciones Económicas).

Aboal, D., F. Lorenzo, and N. Noya, 2003, "La Inflación como Objetivo en Uruguay: Consideraciones sobre los Mecanismos de Transmisión de la Política Monetaria y Cambiaria," Banco Central del Uruguay *Revista de Economía-Segunda Epoca*, Vol. 10 (May), pp. 41–178.

Armas, A., N. Batini, and V. Tuesta, 2007, "Peru's Experience with Partial Dollarization and Inflation Targeting," in *Perú—Selected Issues*, IMF Country Report No. 07/53 (Washington: International Monetary Fund).

Benigno, G., C. Otrok, A. Rebucci, and E. Young, 2007, "Optimal Monetary Policy in a Model with Endogenous Sudden Stops" (unpublished; Washington: International Monetary Fund).

———, forthcoming, "Alternative Monetary Policy Rules in a Model with Endogenous Sudden Stops," in Frontiers of Economics and Globalization series (Amsterdam: North-Holland).

Borensztein, E., M. Chamon, O. Jeanne, P. Mauro, and J. Zettelmeyer, 2004, *Sovereign Debt Structure for Crisis Prevention*, IMF Occasional Paper No. 237 (Washington: International Monetary Fund).

Calvo, G., and F. Mishkin, 2003, "The Mirage of Exchange Rate Regimes for Emerging Market Countries," NBER Working Paper No. 9808 (Cambridge, Massachusetts: National Bureau of Economic Research).

Campa, J.M., and L.S. Goldberg, 2002, "Exchange Rate Pass-Through into Import Prices: A Macro or Micro Phenomenon?" NBER Working Paper No. 8934 (Cambridge, Massachusetts: National Bureau of Economic Research).

de Brun, J., and G. Licandro, 2006, "To Hell and Back. Crisis Management in a Dollarized Economy: The Case of Uruguay," in *Financial Dollarization: The Policy Agenda*, ed. by A. Armas, A. Ize, and E. Levy Yeyati (Washington: International Monetary Fund).

de Brun, J., N. Gandelman, H. Kamil, and A.C. Porzencanski, 2008, "The Fixed-Income Market in Uruguay," in *Bond Markets in Latin America: On the Verge of a Big Bang?* ed. by E. Borenzstein, K. Cowan, B. Eichengreen, and U. Panizza (forthcoming; Cambridge, Massachusetts: MIT Press).

Edwards, S., 2006, "The Relationship Between Exchange Rates and Inflation Targeting Revisited," NBER Working Paper No. 12163 (Cambridge, Massachusetts National Bureau of Economic Research).

Frankel, J.A., D. Parsley, and S-J. Wei, 2005, "Slow Passthrough Around the World: A New Import for Developing Countries?" NBER Working Paper No. 11199 (Cambridge, Massachusetts: National Bureau of Economic Research).

International Monetary Fund, 2003, *Uruguay: 2003 Article IV Consultation*, IMF Country Report No. 03/247 (Washington).

Ize, A., and E. Levy-Yeyati, 2006, "Financial De-Dollarization: Is It for Real?" in *Financial Dollarization: The Policy Agenda*, ed. by A. Armas, A. Ize and E. Levy Yeyati (Washington: International Monetary Fund).

Jeanne, O., 2003, "Why Do Emerging Market Economies Borrow in Foreign Currency?" IMF Working Paper 03/177 (Washington: International Monetary Fund).

Licandro, J.A., 2000, "The Scope for Inflation Targeting in Uruguay" (unpublished; Montevideo: Banco Central de Uruguay).

Masoller, A., 1997, "Una Medición de la Credibilidad de los Programas de Estabilización en Uruguay: 1978–82 y 1990–95," Banco Central del Uruguay *Revista de Economía-Segunda Epoca*, Vol. 4 (May), pp. 73–152.

Mishkin, F., and M. Savastano, 2000, "Monetary Policy Strategies for Latin America," NBER Working Paper No. 7617 (Cambridge, Massachusetts: National Bureau of Economic Research).

Rajan, R., 2004, "Dollar Shortages and Crises," NBER Working Paper No. 10845 (Cambridge, Massachusetts: National Bureau of Economic Research).

Rebucci, A., and M. Rossi, 2006, "Measuring Disinflation Credibility in Emerging Markets: A Bayesian Approach with an Application to Turkey's IMF-Supported Program," *Economics Bulletin*, Vol. 6, No. 11, pp. 1–8.

Taylor, J., 2000, "Low Inflation, Pass-Through, and the Pricing Power of Firms," *European Economic Review*, Vol. 44 (June): pp. 1389–408.

Varela-Loschiavo, G., and C. Vera Iglesias, 2003, "Mecanismos de Transmisión de la Política Monetario-Cambiaria a Precios," Banco Central del Uruguay *Revista de Economía-Segunda Epoca*, Vol. 10 (May), pp. 87–150.

Part 2

External Linkages Under Dollarization

IV Role of Bank Lending in the Transmission of Macroeconomic Shocks

Gaston Gelos and Marco Piñón

More than five years have passed since the banking crisis in Uruguay, and the first signs of a recovery in bank credit are visible (Figure 4.1). In particular, after a continued strong economic expansion since 2003, lending in local currency has picked up recently. Still, credit levels remain distant from precrisis levels. In line with the postcrisis experience of other countries, output has so far been able to recover essentially without bank credit. However, the economy is entering a phase in which formal financial intermediation is likely to become more important to sustain economic activity (Calvo, Izquierdo, and Talvi, 2006). It is therefore important to gain a better understanding of bank credit behavior. What role will the new Uruguayan financial system play in the transmission of foreign and domestic, including monetary, shocks? This question is particularly important given the current reassessment of the monetary policy framework in Uruguay.

This chapter makes use of microeconomic bank data to draw inferences on bank behavior. In addition to the usual identification problems, understanding bank behavior from a time series perspective is challenging given severe structural changes since the 2002 crisis, including the failure of various banks, the creation of a new institution, and the subsequent substantial tightening in regulation and supervision. However, using detailed monthly balance sheet data, this chapter exploits its cross-sectional as well as the time series dimension. First, the chapter tests for the existence of a bank lending channel of monetary transmission for domestic currency loans. Second, it assesses whether similar effects exist for the transmission of international shocks to foreign currency loans.

The chapter finds evidence of the existence of a bank lending channel in local currency loans. In response to a monetary contraction (expansion), banks tend to reduce (expand) their loan supply; in line with the hypothesis on the role of financial frictions, this effect is stronger for less liquid and less

Figure 4.1. Bank Lending in Uruguay

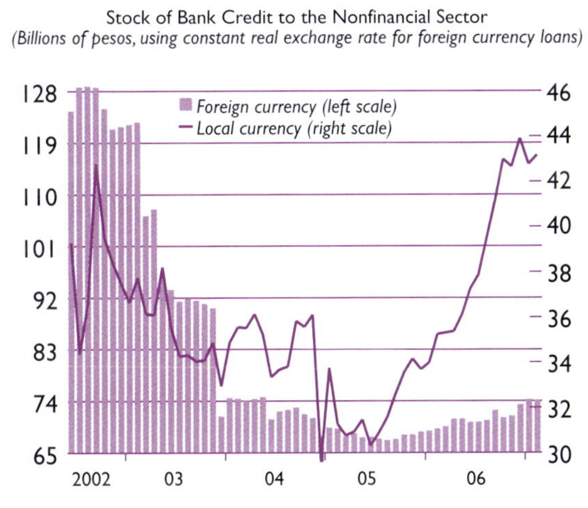

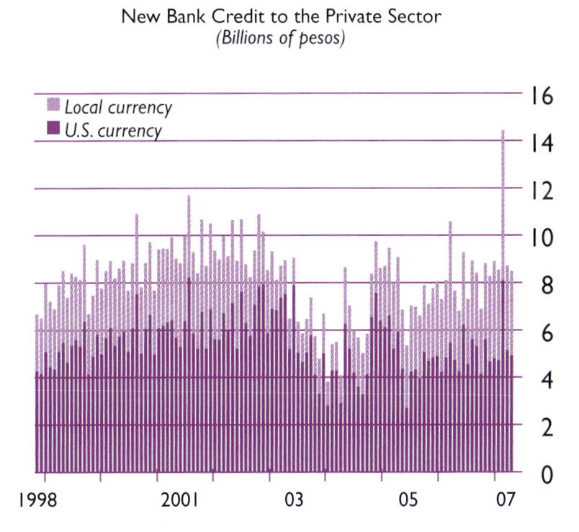

Source: Central Bank of Uruguay.

Table 4.1. Financing Structure of Firms in Uruguay, 2004
(Structure of liabilities, percent of total)

	Bonds	Bank Loans	Suppliers' Credit	Retained Earnings
Median	0	16.1	21.8	38.2
Mean	0.6	26.2	27.8	45.2

Source: de Brun and others (2006).

capitalized banks. This transmission mechanism operates above and beyond other channels, such as the interest rate or exchange rate channel. Its quantitative significance is still somewhat limited given the preponderance of foreign currency lending, but its importance is growing.

Similarly, there is evidence of an equivalent transmission of foreign shocks. More capitalized and liquid banks reduce their lending in foreign currency less strongly in response to U.S. interest hikes. There is no statistically significant difference in the reaction of banks with different degrees of liability dollarization. Together with the findings on the bank lending channel, this implies that, as bank lending picks up and bank liquidity falls, the banking system will tend to amplify domestic and foreign shocks more in the future.

Descriptive Evidence on the Importance of Bank Lending for Economic Activity

Banks have traditionally been an important source of finance for Uruguayan companies. The importance of stock and corporate bond markets is minimal (Table 4.1). In 2007, 10 companies were listed on the stock market, of which 2 were not traded; 23 companies were listed on the corporate bond market. In 2005, only 4 companies issued bonds. Retained earnings remains the most important source of financing for Uruguayan firms. External financing is divided in broadly similar shares among bank loans and suppliers' credit.

Evidence suggests that the cyclical component of credit in Uruguay has been strongly correlated with economic activity. As expected, the correlation is stronger for those sectors that have less access to other sources of finance, such as households and construction (not shown). This illustrative evidence supports the notion that real activity and bank lending are linked in Uruguay; however, it does not allow inferences to be drawn on causality or bank lending behavior because it is unable to disentangle supply and demand effects. Moreover, the significant structural break linked to the 2002 banking crisis, with its associated bank closures and subsequent changes in supervision, hampers the possibility of extrapolating past bank behavior to the future (Figure 4.2).

Banks' Response to Shocks: Microeconomic Evidence

Data

This chapter uses detailed data available on Uruguayan banks, published by the Central Bank of Uruguay. The data contain monthly flow and stock variables; the chapter focuses on the period 2003–06. Summary statistics are presented in Table 4.2. The Uruguayan banking system is characterized by a segmentation between a state bank—BROU (which represents close to 50 percent of total deposits)—and a group of foreign-owned banks. The mortgage bank BHU has been banned from taking deposits and conducting lending since the crisis and, therefore, is not included in the sample.

Is There a Bank Lending Channel?

The bank lending channel assigns a specific role to banks in the transmission mechanisms of monetary policy. The basic hypothesis is that when there is a monetary contraction and banks lose deposits, financial frictions prevent banks from raising funds in an alternative manner (for example, by issuing CDs). As a result, they reduce their lending. If firms, in turn, cannot easily substitute bank credit, this will lead to real effects.[1]

[1]See Bernanke and Gertler (1995) and Bernanke and Blinder (1988). The bank lending channel hypothesis is a specific mechanism within the broader "credit channel hypothesis." The latter states that because of financial frictions, monetary policy affects the external finance premium that firms and banks have to pay to borrow. For an examination of the bank lending channel in a partially dollarized economy, see Mora (2003).

Figure 4.2. Correlations Between Leads and Lags of the Cyclical Components of Credit and GDP

<table>
<tr><th>GDP_CY,
CREDIT_CYC(–i)</th><th>GDP_CY,
CREDIT_CYC(+i)</th><th>i</th><th>Lag</th><th>Lead</th></tr>
<tr><td>. |*** |</td><td>. |*** |</td><td>0</td><td>0.3066</td><td>0.3066</td></tr>
<tr><td>. |**. |</td><td>. |**** |</td><td>1</td><td>0.2382</td><td>0.4274</td></tr>
<tr><td>. |**. |</td><td>. |**** |</td><td>2</td><td>0.1583</td><td>0.4398</td></tr>
<tr><td>. | . |</td><td>. |***** |</td><td>3</td><td>0.0453</td><td>0.4571</td></tr>
<tr><td>.**| . |</td><td>. |**** |</td><td>4</td><td>–0.1561</td><td>0.4127</td></tr>
</table>

Source: IMF staff estimates based on Central Bank of Uruguay data.
Sample: 1988Q1–2002Q1. Included observations: 57. Correlations are asymptotically consistent approximations.

Table 4.2. Selected Indicators of Uruguayan Banks by Type, 2006

(In millions of U.S. dollars, unless otherwise indicated)

	Banks	
	Private	Public (BROU)
Equity	34.2	507.7
Paid-up capital/total assets ratio	4.1	0
Total assets	449.3	5,739.1
Fixed assets	5.1	155.9
Liquid assets/total assets	5.3	9.5
Loans/assets ratio	29.5	22.5
Deposits	403.4	5,083
Loans/deposits ratio	32.8	25.4
Interest revenue	23.9	304.5
Interest expenses	5.9	53.2
Personnel expenses/(Deposits+Loans)	2	1.7
Other operating expenses/ (Deposits+Loans)	0.9	0.6
Number of branches	12	119
Employment	230	3,596
Number of banks	14	1

Source: Central Bank of Uruguay.

Note: Figures are medians (in millions of U.S. dollars except for ratios, branches, employment, and number of banks) for December 2006. Ratios and shares are in percentages. Excludes Banco Hipotecario del Uruguay (BHU).

BROU = Banco de la República Oriental del Uruguay.

This chapter exploits heterogeneity in bank characteristics to test for the existence of a lending channel. Given that credit aggregates are determined jointly by supply and demand, examining correlations between credit and other economic variables does not identify a lending channel. Therefore, the strategy adopted in this literature is to focus on cross-sectional differences in bank behavior: banks that can a priori be expected to be less credit constrained should react less strongly to monetary policy shocks (see, for example, Kashyap and Stein, 2000). This chapter differentiates banks according to their degree of liquidity and capitalization. It is presumed that firms cannot easily substitute bank loans with other sources of external finance, in light of the evidence presented earlier.

Loan growth regressions are estimated using quarterly data with short-term interest rates and changes in the announced growth rate of M0/M1 as monetary policy variables. To obtain a measure of truly exogenous monetary policy shocks, the chapter first regresses the change in each of these domestic monetary variables on changes in U.S. interest rates and Latin American

Table 4.3. Differential Response of Local Currency Loan Growth to Monetary Policy Shocks by Bank Characteristic

	Differential Impact by Bank Characteristic	
Monetary Policy Variable	Liquidity	Capitalization
Δi	–0.015***	–0.024**
Δi x bank characteristic	0.0015***	1.094***
ΔM	0.244***	0.0932
ΔM x bank characteristic	–0.003***	–1.604***

Source: IMF staff estimates.

Note: Estimation period is 2003:Q1–2006:Q4. Quarterly data, two lags. Long-term coefficients are reported. Based on generalized least squares estimation with bank fixed effects and time effects, allowing for correlation of errors and correcting for serial correlation. Control variables are manufacturing growth, exchange rate change, change in country risk, change in inflation expectations. Does not include Banco de la República Oriental del Uruguay (BROU) (including BROU yields similar results). Δi and ΔM (predicted), refer to the fitted values of a regression of domestic interest changes on the Latin Emerging Market Bond Index spread and U.S. interest rates.

Emerging Market Bond Index (EMBI) spreads and then uses the predicted values of these regressions. Dynamic regressions are estimated using manufacturing growth, exchange rate change, change in country risk, and change in inflation expectations as control variables. Time dummies are also used as alternatives. The estimations are carried out with bank dummies, allowing for bank-specific heterogeneity, for correlation of contemporaneous errors, and correcting for first-order serial correlation.[2]

$$\begin{aligned}\Delta\log(Loans_{it}) = & \sum_{j=1}^{m}\alpha_j\Delta\log(Loans_{it-j}) \\ & + \sum_{j=0}^{m} b_j\Delta MonetaryVariable \\ & + \sum_{j=0}^{m} c_j\Delta MonetaryVariable \\ & \cdot BankChar + d \cdot BankChar_{t-1} \\ & + \sum_{j=0}^{m} e\Delta ControlVar_j + \mu_i + \varepsilon_{it}. \qquad (1)\end{aligned}$$

The results support the existence of a bank lending channel for local currency loans. In line with this hypothesis, it is found that more liquid and more capitalized banks do react less strongly to monetary policy shocks (Table 4.3). For example, a 1 percent increase in the short-term interest rate yields an average drop in the quarterly growth rate in local currency credit of about 2 percent (compared with a median growth rate of 5 percent in the sample). A bank at the top 80th percentile in liquidity ratio, however, would not significantly change its lending. As expected, the bank lending channel effects cannot be confirmed statistically for overall loans, given the large share of dollar loans. With the share of peso credit growing, the bank lending channel will be gaining quantitative importance in Uruguay.

The growing importance of the bank lending channel brings opportunities and challenges. Although the effectiveness of monetary policy is enhanced through this additional mechanism, the amplification of monetary shocks implies the need for a more fine-tuned policy. Moreover, as banks continue to lend more, their current high liquidity levels are likely to fall, further amplifying their responses.

Transmission of Foreign Shocks

Does a similar mechanism operate in the transmission of foreign shocks? To answer this question, the chapter explores a similar specification with a focus on the transmission of foreign shocks. In particular, it examines the effects of changes of U.S. interest rates on foreign currency lending behavior, by type of bank.

More liquid banks and those with fewer dollar liabilities reduce their lending less strongly in response to U.S. interest hikes. An increase in U.S. interest rates is associated with a drop in lending—a 100-basis-point increase yields a drop in the quarterly growth rate of 9 percentage points (Table 4.4). This effect is milder for more liquid and better capitalized banks. There is no statistically significant difference in the reaction of banks with different degrees of capitalization.

[2]Given the presence of a lagged dependent variable, a generalized method of moments estimation following Arellano and Bond (1991) or Arellano and Bover (1995) could be considered. We do not pursue this here because the cross-sectional dimension of the panel is small; moreover, we are not interested in the coefficient on the dependent variable.

Table 4.4. Differential Response of Foreign Currency Loan Growth to Foreign Shocks

	Differential Impact by Bank Characteristic		
Foreign Shock	Dollarization of liabilities	Liquidity	Capitalization
Δi US	–0.09***	–0.12***	–0.06***
Δi US x bank characteristic	–0.34***	0.002***	–0.154

Source: IMF staff estimates.

Note: Estimation period is 2003:Q1–2006:Q4. Quarterly data, two lags. Long-term coefficients are reported. Based on generalized least squares estimation with bank fixed effects and time effects, allowing for correlation of errors and correcting for serial correlation. Includes Banco de la República Oriental del Uruguay.

Conclusions

The results indicate that bank lending in local currency reacts to changes in domestic monetary policy. This suggests that monetary policy will become more effective over time, but also more challenging. With a growing share of peso-denominated debt, the bank lending channel will become more important. This means that monetary policy shocks will be amplified, which in turn implies that its fine-tuning will become more relevant.

The results also show that domestic credit in foreign currency is partly driven by foreign shocks. Moreover, the less liquid banks are, the more foreign and domestic shocks are amplified. With the ongoing resumption in lending, banks' liquidity will naturally decline from their current high levels. This will further amplify the effect of shocks in the future, implying the need for more vigilance in macroeconomic policies.

Bibliography

Arellano, Manuel, and Stephen Bond, 1991, "Some Tests of Specification for Panel Data: Monte Carlo Evidence and an Application to Employment Equations," *Review of Economic Studies*, Vol. 58 (April), pp. 277–97.

Arellano, Manuel, and Olympia Bover, 1995, "Another Look at the Instrumental Variable Estimation of Error-Components Models," *Journal of Econometrics*, Vol. 68 (July), pp. 29–51.

Arena, Marco, Carmen Reinhart, and Francisco Vázquez, 2006, "The Lending Channel in Emerging Economics: Are Foreign Banks Different?" NBER Working Paper No. 12340 (Cambridge, Massachusetts: National Bureau of Research).

Bernanke, Ben S., and Alan S. Blinder, 1988, "Credit, Money, and Aggregate Demand," *American Economic Review Papers and Proceedings*, Vol. 78 (May), pp. 435–39.

Bernanke, Ben S., and Mark Gertler, 1995, "Inside the Black Box: The Credit Channel of Monetary Policy Transmission," *Journal of Economic Perspectives*, Vol. 9 (Autumn), pp. 27–48.

Calvo, Guillermo A., Alejandro Izquierdo, and Ernesto Talvi, 2006, "Phoenix Miracles in Emerging Markets: Recovering Without Credit from Systemic Financial Crises," Research Department Working Paper No. 570 (Washington: Inter-American Development Bank). Available via the Internet: www.iadb.org/res/files/Imbalances/pp/CALVO-IZQUIERDO-TALVI.pdf

Chiesa, Pablo, Paula Gara, and María José Zerbino, 2004, "Efectos Reales de la Política Monetaria en Uruguay: Una Aproximación al Estudio de los Canales de la Tasa de Interés y del Crédito Bancario" (Master's thesis; Montevideo: Universidad de la República, Uruguay).

de Brun, Julio, Néstor Gandelman, and Eduardo Barbieri, 2003, "Investment and Financial Restrictions at the Firm Level in Uruguay," in *Credit Constraints and Investment in Latin America*, ed. by Arturo Galindo and Fabio Schiantarelli (Washington: Inter-American Development Bank).

de Brun, Julio, Néstor Gandelman, Herman Kamil, and Arturo Porzecanski, 2006, "The Fixed-Income Market in Uruguay" (unpublished; Montevideo: Universidad ORT Uruguay).

International Monetary Fund, 2006, *Uruguay: Financial Sector Stability Assessment*, IMF Country Report No. 06/439 (Washington).

Kashyap, Anil K., and Jeremy C. Stein, 2000, "What Do a Million Observations on Banks Say About the Transmission of Monetary Policy?" *American Economic Review*, Vol. 90 (June), pp. 407–28.

Mora, Nada, 2003, "The Bank-Lending Channel in a Partially Dollarized Economy" (unpublished; Beirut: The American University of Beirut)

Takeda, Tony, Fabiana Rocha, and Marcio I. Nakane, 2005, "The Reaction of Bank Lending to Monetary Policy in Brazil," *Revista Brasileira de Economia*, Vol. 59, No. 1.

V What Is the Degree of Competition Intensity in the Uruguayan Banking System?

Gaston Gelos and Marco Piñón

From a medium-term growth perspective, it is important to understand the role of structural factors in shaping the behavior of the financial system in Uruguay. Although previous work suggests that—at least until recently—credit is not supply-constrained, it is worthwhile to assess whether looking forward there are any institutional factors that could hinder the further deepening of sound financial intermediation in Uruguay (see Canales-Kriljenko and Gelos, 2006).

Until before the crisis, credit levels relative to GDP in Uruguay were broadly in line with Latin American averages but low by international standards. In the 1990s, bank credit to the private sector fluctuated around 30 percent, comparable to the levels in Argentina, Brazil, and Colombia—but below OECD levels of about 70 percent (Beck and Levine, 2004) and those of other emerging markets. Currently, the ratio of credit to GDP in Uruguay stands at 25 percent (Figure 5.1).

Cross-country empirical evidence suggests that growth prospects in Uruguay would be further enhanced through deeper financial intermediation. A causal link from financial intermediation to growth has been empirically established in the literature. The evidence stems largely from cross-country regressions using proper instrumental variable procedures to avoid endogeneity problems (for example, Levine, 2003). The results indicate that financial development affects growth by increasing productivity rather than capital accumulation (see Beck, Levine, and Loayza, 2000; and IMF, 2004). Evidence from panel regressions presented in Beck,

Figure 5.1. Bank Credit to the Private Sector in Selected Countries
(In percent of GDP)

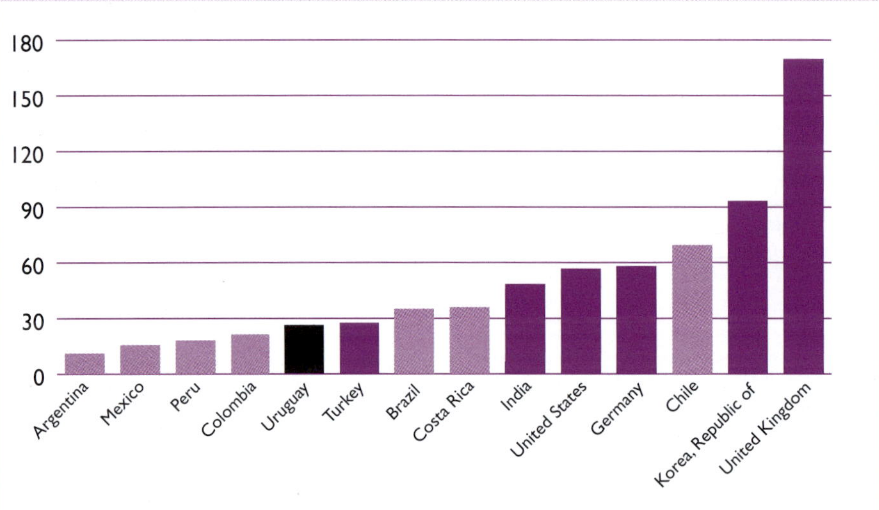

Source: IMF, *International Financial Statistics*.

Figure 5.2. Concentration Index
(Based on shares of total deposits)

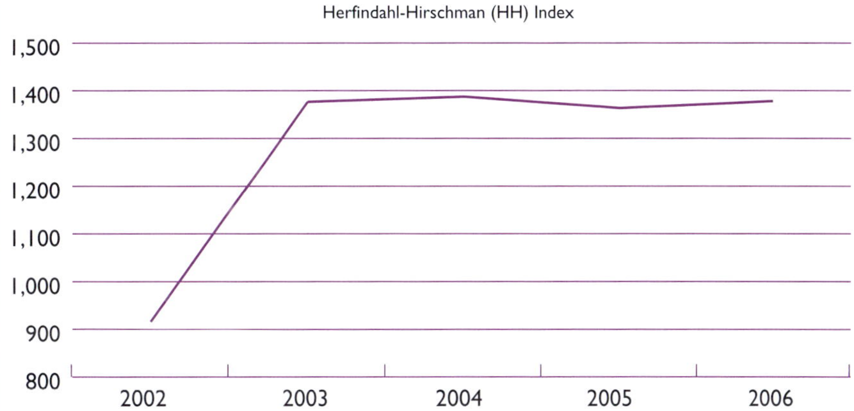

Source: IMF staff estimates based on Central Bank of Uruguay data.

Levine, and Loayza (2000) suggests that if bank credit in Uruguay could be exogenously raised from 30 to 35 percent, average yearly GDP growth could be 0.4 percent higher. Nevertheless, these conceptual experiments are only illustrative, with the more relevant question being how to increase financial development (Levine, 2003).

To assess prospects for increased financial intermediation, the paper examines competitive conditions in the banking sector. International evidence shows that higher banking competition is associated with lower spreads and easier access to finance by companies (Beck, Demirguç-Kunt, and Maksimovic, 2004; and Gelos, 2006). The degree of competition may also matter from a cyclical perspective, because it has been argued that imperfect competition in the banking sector may propagate external shocks and amplify swings (Mandelman, 2006).[1]

Assessing the Degree of Competition

Concentration in the Uruguayan banking system has risen. The number of banks has declined during and after the crisis, and the market concentration has increased, as measured by Herfindahl-Hirschman (HH) indices (Figure 5.2). The index is now close to 1,400. As a comparison, Gelos and Roldós (2004) report HH indices for 13 emerging markets; in their sample, the median HH index in 2000 was 900, and the median in Latin America 923.

The banking system is characterized by relatively low competition intensity. Some indicators suggest that competition is low relative to other countries and that it has, if anything, been decreasing. This raises the challenge of strengthening competition intensity without endangering financial stability.

A market structure test based on reduced form revenue functions was used to assess the degree of competition intensity. Panzar and Rosse (1987) show that the sum of the elasticities of a firm's revenue with respect to the firm's input prices (the so-called H statistic) can be used to identify the nature of the market structure in which the firm operates. In long-run competitive equilibrium, the H statistic should be equal to one as increases in input prices should lead to a one-to-one increase in total revenues. By contrast, the H will be negative if the firm operates as a monopoly—an upward shift in the marginal cost curve will be associated with a reduction in revenue as a result of the optimality condition for the monopolist (Table 5.1). Under monopolistic competition, the H statistic will lie between zero and one. If the elasticity of demand is constant, then there is a monotone relationship between the mark-up over marginal costs—a measure of the degree of competition—and the H index. More formally, letting R denote a revenue function of input prices w and exogenous variables z,

[1]Regarding the relationship between competition and financial stability, the evidence is not conclusive (see, for example, the discussion in Drummond, Maechler, and Marcelino, 2007).

Table 5.1. Panzar and Rosse's *H* Statistic

Market Structure	
$H<0$	Monopoly [or conjectural variation oligopoly]
$0<H<1$	Monopolistic competition
$H=1$	Perfect competition or monopoly in a perfectly contestable market

Source: Panzar and Rosse (1987).

$$R = R(w,z)$$

$$H = \sum_i \frac{\partial R^*}{\partial w_i} \frac{w_i}{R_i}. \qquad (1)$$

This approach has been widely applied to banking systems. Early studies examine competitive conditions in the United States and Canada (see Shaffer, 1989; and Nathan and Neave, 1989, respectively).[2] Under this methodology, banks are treated as single-product firms (De Bandt and Davis, 2000). In this approach, banks produce intermediation services using labor and capital as inputs (see Freixas and Rochet, 1997).[3]

To derive the H statistic, the paper estimates the following reduced form revenue equation:

$$\ln IR = c + a \cdot \ln w_L + b \cdot \ln w_F + c \cdot \ln w_K + d \cdot cap + e \cdot oth, \qquad (2)$$

where

IR = interest revenue (or interest revenue divided by total assets)
c = constant
w_L = unit price of labor
w_F = unit price of funds
w_K = unit price of capital
cap = capacity indicators, such as total fixed assets

[2]For studies of European countries, see Molyneux, Lloyd-Williams, and Thornton (1994); Bikker and Groeneveld (2000); and De Bandt and Davis (2000). For a study covering various emerging markets, see Gelos and Roldós (2004). Individual country studies include, among others, Austria (Mooslechner and Schnitzer, 1995), Brazil (Belaisch, 2003), Bulgaria (Feyzioğlu and Gelos, 2000), Colombia (Barajas, Steiner, and Salazar, 2000), Italy (Coccorese, 1998), Switzerland (Rime, 1999), Germany (Lang, 1997; and Hempell, 2002), Japan (Molyneux, Thornton, and Lloyd-Williams, 1996), and Finland (Vesala, 1995).

[3]However, product differentiation is allowed for in the monopolistic competition model.

Table 5.2. Results from Revenue Estimations

	(1) ln*IR*	(2) ln*rev*	(3) ln*IR*	(4) ln*rev*
ln (wages)	0.269	0.265	0.269	0.267
	(2.17)*	(2.00)*	(2.15)*	(2.00)*
ln (cost of funds)	0.252	0.233	0.250	0.232
	(3.48)**	(3.41)**	(3.45)**	(3.39)**
ln (cost of capital)	0.260	0.230	0.259	0.224
	(3.58)***	(3.21)**	(3.04)**	(2.57)**
ln (wages) x after	–0.038	–0.038	–0.039	–0.039
	(0.85)	(0.96)	(0.84)	(0.96)
ln (cost of capital) x after	–0.193	–0.186	–0.193	–0.188
	(3.07)**	(3.20)**	(3.04)**	(3.15)**
ln (cost of funds) x after	–0.023	–0.021	–0.023	–0.022
	(0.43)	(0.48)	(0.43)	(0.48)
Loans/total assets	1.404	1.318	1.434	1.344
	(3.91)***	(3.94)***	(3.98)***	(4.00)***
ln (total assets)	0.977	1.065	0.972	1.062
	(8.67)***	(9.79)***	(8.67)***	(9.76)***
Number of observations	88	88	84	84
R^2	0.98	0.98	0.97	0.97
H 2003–04	0.78	0.73	0.78	0.72
Change in *H*	–0.25*	–0.25*	–0.25	–0.25*
H 2005–06	0.53	0.48	0.52	0.47

Source: IMF staff estimates.

Notes: *IR* is interest revenue; *rev* is total revenues. After = Dummy for period since 2005, includes bank fixed effects. Standard errors are adjusted for clustering by date. * Denotes significance at the 10 percent confidence level; ** significance at 5 percent; *** significance at 1 percent.

oth = other factors potentially affecting interest revenues, such as the business mix of the bank, the size of total assets (to control for scale effects), and nonperforming loans

Equation (2) is estimated using semiannual data for 2003–06. The unit cost of labor is proxied by salary expenses over personnel, the unit cost of funds by interest payments over deposits, and the unit cost of capital by other expenses divided by total fixed assets. Tests are also conducted for changes in the H statistic between 2003–04 and 2005–06 (Table 5.2).

The estimates suggest that the banking system is characterized by monopolistic competition. With the H statistic around 0.5, the estimation indicates that the degree of competition intensity is low by international standards. In a study of 50 countries, Claessens and Laeven (2004) report H statistics around 0.6–0.8, with a median value close to 0.7. Although cross-country comparisons of these statistics are problematic, the finding of low competition confirms the results of Mello Costa (2006), who uses a different approach and does not look at changes over time. A caveat is that the standard errors are large; therefore, the measurement is not very precise.

Along with the rise in concentration, competition has tended to decrease since the crisis. The estimates show a drop in H since 2005, albeit only at low significance levels. Nevertheless, the more recent estimates may be more valid because the banking system is likely to be operating under conditions more closely resembling those of a long-run equilibrium.

The results suggest that increasing competition in the banking system without jeopardizing financial stability is an important challenge for Uruguay. Although a discussion of concrete policy measures in this area would exceed the scope of the paper, leveling the playing field between private and public banks would likely contribute to this objective (see Mello Costa, 2006; and IMF, 2006).

Conclusions

From a structural perspective, the study indicates that measures to promote a more competitive environment are likely to enhance sustained growth over the medium term. In particular, it finds that the degree of competition in the Uruguayan banking system is relatively low by international standards. Looking ahead, this may limit financial deepening and, thereby, economic growth. Thus, a challenge for the authorities is to foster healthy competition further while preserving the soundness of the financial system.

Bibliography

Arellano, Manuel, and Stephen Bond, 1991, "Some Tests of Specification for Panel Data: Monte Carlo Evidence and an Application to Employment Equations," *Review of Economic Studies*, Vol. 58 (April), pp. 277–97.

Arellano, Manuel, and Olympia Bover, 1995, "Another Look at the Instrumental Variable Estimation of Error-Components Models," *Journal of Econometrics*, Vol. 68 (July), pp. 29–51.

Barajas, Adolfo, Roberto Steiner, and Natalia Salazar, 2000, "The Impact of Liberalization and Foreign Investment in Colombia's Financial Sector," *Journal of Development Economics*, Vol. 63 (October), pp. 157–96.

Beck, Thorsten, Asli Demirguç-Kunt, and Vojislav Maksimovic, 2004, "Bank Competition and Access to Finance: International Evidence," *Journal of Money, Credit and Banking*, Vol. 36 (June), pp. 627–48.

Beck, Thorsten, and Ross Levine, 2004, "Stock Markets, Banks, and Growth: Panel Evidence," *Journal of Banking and Finance*, Vol. 28 (March), pp. 423–42.

———, and Norman Loayza, 2000, "Finance and the Sources of Growth," *Journal of Financial Economics*, Vol. 58, No. 1–2, pp. 261–300.

Belaisch, Agnes, 2003, "Do Brazilian Banks Compete?" IMF Working Paper 03/113 (Washington: International Monetary Fund).

Bikker, Jacob A., and J.M. Groeneveld, 2000, "Competition and Concentration in the EU Banking Industry," *Kredit und Kapital*, No. 1, pp. 62–98.

Canales-Kriljenko, Jorge, and Gaston Gelos, 2006, "Post-Crisis Credit: Facts, Lessons, and Prospects," in *Uruguay: Selected Issues*, IMF Country Report No. 06/427 (Washington: International Monetary Fund).

Claessens, Stijn, and Luc Laeven, 2004, "What Drives Bank Competition? Some International Evidence," *Journal of Money, Credit and Banking*, Vol. 36 (June, Part 2), pp. 563–83.

Coccorese, Paolo, 1998, "Assessing the Competitive Conditions in the Italian Banking System: Some Empirical Evidence," *BNL Quarterly Review*, No. 205, pp. 171–91.

De Bandt, O., and E.P. Davis, 2000, "Competition, Contestability and Market Structure in European Banking Sectors on the Eve of EMU," *Journal of Banking and Finance*, Vol. 24 (June), pp. 1045–66.

de Brun, Julio, Néstor Gandelman, and Eduardo Barbieri, 2003, "Investment and Financial Restrictions at the Firm Level in Uruguay," in *Credit Constraints and Investment in Latin America*, ed. by Arturo Galindo and Fabio Schiantarelli (Washington: Inter-American Development Bank).

de Brun, Julio, Néstor Gandelman, Herman Kamil, and Arturo Porzecanski, 2006, "The Fixed-Income Market in Uruguay" (unpublished; Montevideo: Universidad ORT Uruguay).

Drummond, Paulo, Andrea M. Maechler, and Sandra Marcelino, 2007, "Italy—Assessing Competition and Efficiency in the Banking System," IMF Working Paper 07/26 (Washington: International Monetary Fund).

Feyzioğlu, Tarhan, and R. Gaston Gelos, 2000, "Why Is Private Sector Credit So Low in Bulgaria?" in *Bulgaria—Selected Issues and Statistical Appendix*, IMF Country Report No. 00/54 (Washington: International Monetary Fund).

Freixas, Xavier, and Jean-Charles Rochet, 1997, *Microeconomics of Banking* (Cambridge, Massachusetts: MIT Press).

Gelos, R. Gaston, 2006, "Banking Spreads in Latin America," IMF Working Paper 06/44 (Washington: International Monetary Fund).

———, and Jorge Roldós, 2004, "Consolidation and Market Structure in Emerging Market Banking Systems," *Emerging Markets Review*, Vol. 5 (March), pp. 39–59.

Hempell, Hannah S., 2002, "Testing for Competition Among German Banks," Economic Research Centre Discussion Paper No. 04/02 (Frankfurt am Main: Deutsche Bundesbank). Available via the Internet: opus.zbw-kiel.de/volltexte/2006/4169/pdf/200204dkp.pdf.

International Monetary Fund, 2004, *World Economic Outlook*, World Economic and Financial Surveys (Washington, April).

———, 2006, *Uruguay: Financial Sector Stability Assessment*, IMF Country Report No. 06/439 (Washington).

Kashyap, Anil K., and Jeremy C. Stein, 2000, "What Do a Million Observations on Banks Say About the Transmission of Monetary Policy?" *American Economic Review*, Vol. 90 (June), pp. 407–28.

Lang, G., 1997, "Wettbewerbsverhalten Deutscher Banken: Eine Panelanalyse auf Basis der Rosse-Panzar Statistik," *Jahrbuch der Wirtschaftswissenschaften—Review of Economics*, Vol. 48, No. 1, pp. 21–38.

Levine, Ross, 2003, "More on Finance and Growth: More Finance, More Growth?" Federal Reserve Bank of St. Louis *Review* (July/August), pp. 31–46.

Mandelman, Federico S., 2006, "Business Cycles and Monetary Regimes in Emerging Economies: A Role for a Monopolistic Banking Sector," Working Paper 2006–17 (Atlanta: Federal Reserve Bank of Atlanta). Available via the Internet: www.frbatlanta.org/frbatlanta/filelegacydocs/wp0617.pdf.

Martinez Peria, M.S., A. Powell, and I. Vladkova-Hollar, 2005, "Banking on Foreigners: The Behavior of International Bank Claims on Latin America, 1985–2000," *IMF Staff Papers*, Vol. 52 (September), pp. 430–61.

Mello Costa, Miguel, 2006, "Midiendo la Concentración y el Poder de Mercado en el Sector Bancario Uruguayo: 2003–2005" (unpublished; Montevideo: Central Bank of Uruguay). Available via the Internet: www.bcu.gub.uy/autoriza/peiees/jor/2006/iees03j3100806.pdf.

Micco, Alejandro, and Ugo Panizza, 2006, "Bank Ownership and Lending Behavior," Working Paper No. 369 (Santiago: Central Bank of Chile). Available via the Internet: www.bcentral.cl/estudios/documentos-trabajo/pdf/dtbc369.pdf.

Molyneux, Philip, D.M. Lloyd-Williams, and John Thornton, 1994, "Competitive Conditions in European Banking," *Journal of Banking and Finance*, Vol. 18 (May), pp. 445–59.

Molyneux, Philip, John Thornton, and D. Michael Lloyd-Williams, 1996, "Competition and Market Contestability in Japanese Commercial Banking," *Journal of Economics and Business*, Vol. 48 (February), pp. 33–45.

Mooslechner, P., and Y. Schnitzer, 1995, "Structure-Performance in Banking: An Application to a Typical Universal Banking System," in *Applied Industrial Organization: Towards a Theory Based Empirical Industrial Organization*, ed. by K. Aiginger and J. Finsinger (Dordrecht, Netherlands: Kluwer Academic Publishers), pp. 167–86.

Nathan, A., and E.H. Neave, 1989, "Competition and Contestability in Canada's Financial System: Empirical Results," *Canadian Journal of Economics*, Vol. 22 (August), pp. 576–94.

Panzar, J.C., and J.N. Rosse, 1987, "Testing for 'Monopoly' Equilibrium," *Journal of Industrial Economics*, Vol. 35 (June), pp. 443–56.

Rime, Bertrand, 1999, "Mesure du degré de concurrence dans le systeme bancaire suisse a l'aide du modele de Panzar et Rosse," *Revue Suisse d'Economie Politique et de Statistique*, Vol. 135, No.1, pp. 21–40.

Schaeck, Klaus, Martin Čihák, and Simon Wolfe, 2006, "Are More Competitive Banking Systems More Stable?" IMF Working Paper 06/143 (Washington: International Monetary Fund).

Shaffer S., 1989, "Competition in the U.S. Banking Industry," *Economic Letters*, Vol. 29, No. 4, pp. 321–23.

Vesala, Jukka, 1995, "Testing Competition in Banking: Behavioral Evidence from Finland," Scientific Monograph No. E:1 (Helsinki: Bank of Finland).

Wachtel, Paul, 2003, "How Much Do We Really Know About Growth and Finance?" Federal Reserve Bank of Atlanta *Economic Review* (First Quarter), pp. 33–47.

VI What Drives Uruguayan Sovereign Spreads? The Role of Global Factors and Regional Spillovers

Gustavo Adler and Stephanie Eble

This chapter examines the determinants of Uruguayan sovereign spreads. In particular, it analyzes to what extent sovereign spreads have been driven by economic fundamentals or by external factors. It also assesses the relationship between the spreads of Uruguay and those of other emerging market economies—including neighboring countries—and the change in such a relationship since the 2002 crisis.

The evidence suggests that, although fundamentals explain part of the variance of sovereign spreads, external factors also play an important role. Moreover, there is evidence of external factors becoming more important since the 2002–03 financial crisis. In particular, during the late 1990s Uruguay was perceived as a safe haven in the region and displayed lower sovereign spreads that were largely insulated from regional and emerging market economy shocks, but since the crisis, its spreads have remained at the level of and co-moved closely with those of neighboring countries. Furthermore, econometric estimates point to heightened financial spillovers from other emerging market economies and a change in investors' perception of Uruguay's vulnerability to financial shocks emanating from other emerging market economies. This structural break seems to be associated with the loss of investment grade[1] as evidenced by the decoupling of Uruguayan and Chilean spreads (an investment-grade economy) and a stronger co-movement with non-investment-grade spreads.

Recent important achievements have gone a long way in reducing vulnerabilities, although further efforts are needed. Rapidly improving fundamentals—supported by prudent policies and a benign external environment—have reduced external vulnerabilities and allowed for subsequent credit rating upgrades. However, Uruguay has not yet regained its safe haven status in the region or delinked its fortunes from those of other emerging market economies. Continuing to strengthen the macroeconomic framework, implementing pending structural reforms, and regaining investment grade status will be key to insulate Uruguay from a possible deterioration in global conditions and from future regional shocks.

Stylized Facts

During the late 1990s, Uruguay's sovereign spreads were largely insulated from financial shocks in other emerging market economies. They remained significantly below those of neighboring countries—averaging about 500 basis points (bps) less than the Latin American Emerging Markets Bond Index (EMBI) during 1998–2001—and were only weakly correlated with them. This is likely to have reflected Uruguay's investment grade and the general perception of Uruguay as a safe haven for investment in the region (Figure 6.1). A similar pattern is found when Uruguay's sovereign spreads are compared with the global EMBI.

In 2002–03, Uruguay's sovereign spreads spiked in the midst of the financial crisis rooted in the withdrawal of Argentine deposits from the Uruguayan banking system. A severe contraction of the economy, a depreciation of the peso, and a marked increase in public debt led to debt sustainability concerns and to sharp increases in sovereign spreads to above 2,000 bps. With the voluntary debt restructuring—which did not imply any hair cut, but a small NPV (net present value) reduction—some measure of market confidence was rapidly restored. Still, sovereign spreads remained significantly above precrisis levels, reflecting continued concerns about Uruguay's repayment capacity and the loss of investment-grade rating. Since then, however, spreads have continued a sharp downward trend, reaching precrisis levels by end-2005. This has allowed the government to tap markets at very favorable rates and to improve the profile of public debt significantly.

The marked fall in sovereign spreads has been accompanied by significant improvements in country fundamentals. Strong fiscal consolidation, high output growth, and the recovery of the real exchange rate from its postcrisis lows have contributed to a sharp

[1] In the remainder of the paper, credit ratings refer to foreign currency long-term debt.

Figure 6.1. Uruguay, Latin America and Global Emerging Markets Bond Index (EMBI) Spreads, 1996–2006[1]
(In basis points (bps))

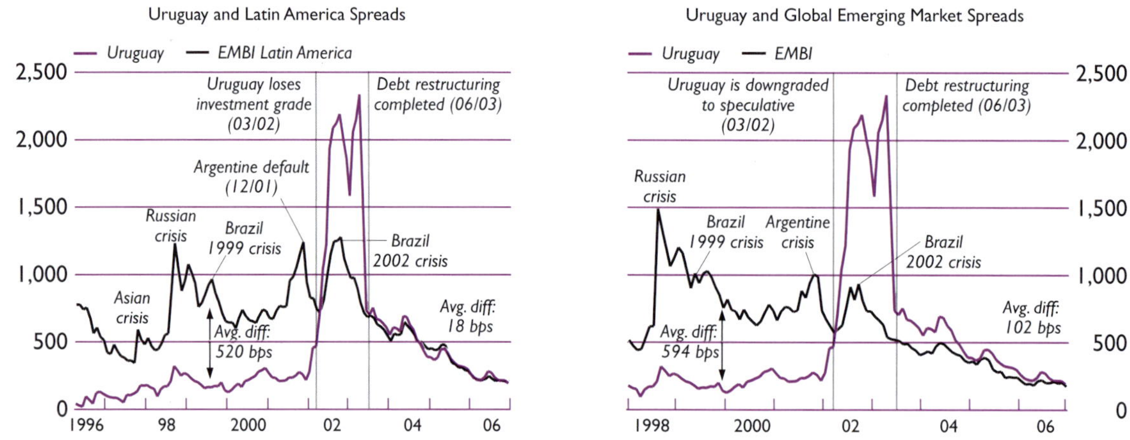

Sources: JPMorgan Chase & Co.; and República AFAP.
[1]For Uruguay, the Uruguayan Bond Index (UBI) is reported; for Latin American and global emerging markets, the JPMorgan EMBI spread is reported.

reduction of public debt as a share of GDP, alleviating solvency concerns. In addition, liquidity indicators have improved substantially, with reserve coverage of short-term external debt and foreign currency deposits well above precrisis levels, partly reflecting a sharp reduction in short-term debt and a marked increase in reserve holdings (Figure 6.2). Furthermore, the recovery of the financial system has reduced contingent fiscal liabilities.

At the same time, Uruguay has benefited from a very benign global environment. Global financial conditions have improved markedly since 2002, up until end-2006. Long-term U.S. interest rates have declined significantly, financial market volatility—a proxy for liquidity conditions—has reached historical lows, and U.S. corporate high-yield spreads have also fallen.[2] Reflecting this favorable environment, emerging market sovereign spreads have followed a steady downward trend across the board, reaching historical lows in 2006.[3]

However, in contrast with the 1990s, since the crisis, Uruguayan spreads have remained close to and have displayed high correlation with neighboring countries' spreads. In particular since 2002, Uruguayan spreads have remained at about the level of and closely co-moved with the Latin American EMBI. Sovereign spread correlations across countries have generally increased—pointing to common factors—but Uruguay has been particularly affected (Figure 6.3). Although daily correlation with neighboring countries was low before the crisis, Uruguayan cross-border correlations increased after the crisis to the levels displayed by other countries in the region (Table 6.1).[4] Notably, correlations with the Latin American EMBI and the global EMBI have tripled. Interestingly, whereas the correlations between Uruguayan and other non-investment-grade Latin American countries' spreads have increased, the correlation with Chile (an investment-grade economy) has declined.

Furthermore, there is evidence of heightened financial spillover risks following the crisis. *Before the crisis,* Uruguayan spreads were relatively insulated from

[2]Financial market volatility is proxied by the Chicago Board Options Exchange Volatility Index, a popular measure of the implied volatility of Standard & Poor's 500 index options, which aggregates market expectations of volatility over the next 30-day period. The Merrill Lynch high-yield index is used to measure the average spread of U.S. speculative grade corporate bonds (a proxy for investor risk appetite).

[3]During the 2007 market turbulence (born in mature economies) emerging market sovereign spreads widened somewhat but remained low relative to historical averages.

[4]Following Forbes and Rigobon (1999) and Gelos and Sahay (2001), a formal test of increase in correlation, applying the correction for changes in variance, was conducted, confirming the findings. As the variance has fallen in the postcrisis period, the adjustment accentuates the increase in correlations.

Figure 6.2. Country Fundamentals and External Factors, 1996–2006

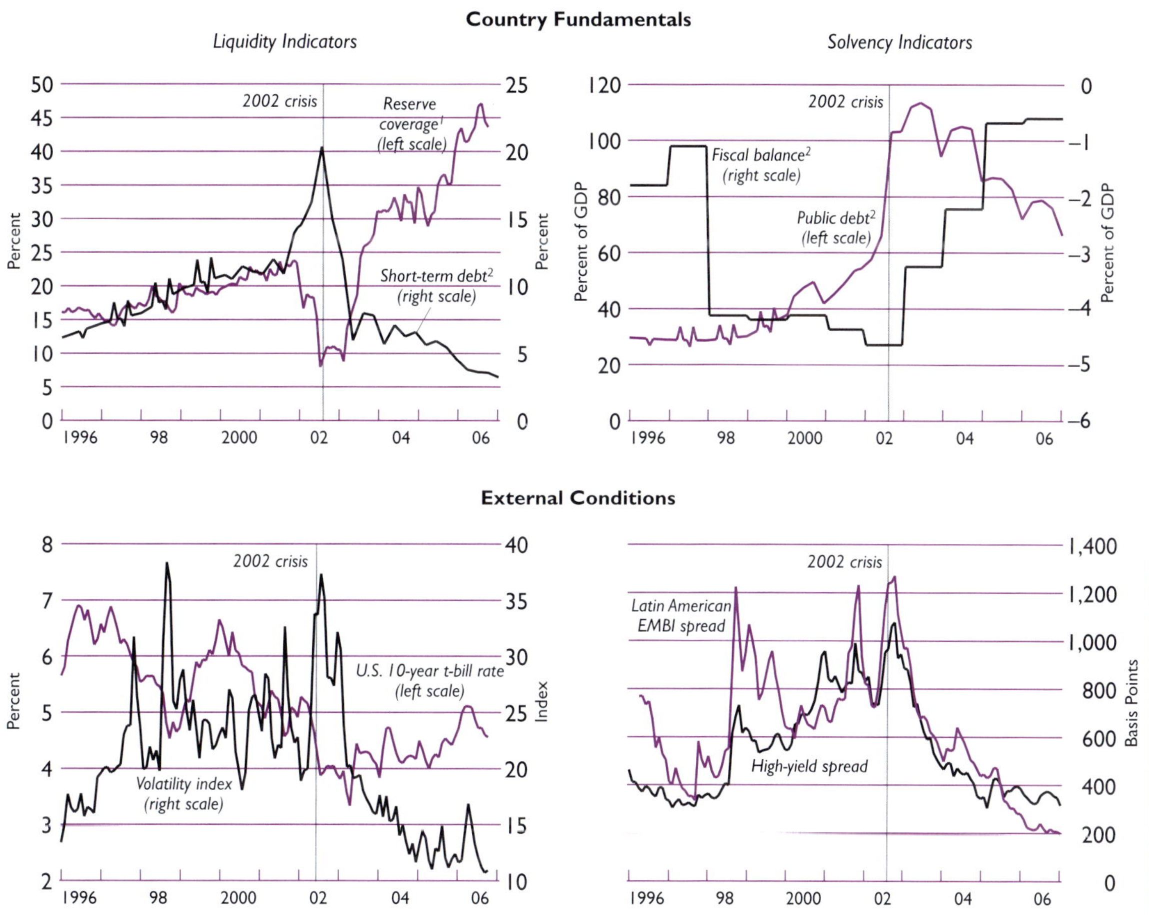

Sources: Bloomberg; Central Bank of Uruguay; and IMF.
[1]Gross international reserves over short-term external debt and foreign currency deposits.
[2]As percent of GDP.

shocks in other countries in the region, as confirmed by Granger causality tests between Uruguayan and Latin American spreads based on daily data (Table 6.2). With exception of Argentina—with which Uruguay had strong trade and financial links—changes in neighboring countries' spreads did not spill over to Uruguay (see Eble, 2006). Most notably, the Brazilian and Latin American EMBIs had no significant effect on Uruguayan spreads.[5] *After the crisis*, however, financial spillovers from the region and other emerging market economies seem to have increased. All pairwise tests show significant causality, pointing to tighter regional and global linkages.[6] It is worth noting, however, that the spike of Argentine spreads, relative to other spreads in the region, during 2007 did not spill over to Uruguayan spreads, suggesting that a process of decoupling from this close neighbor—possibly associated with declining financial and trade links—may be under way, although it is premature to draw conclusions.

[5]It is also interesting to note the impact of Uruguayan shocks on Chilean spreads (at 10 percent significance level) in the precrisis period and the following reversion in the direction of causality after the crisis.

[6]Because the table displays pairwise tests, results should be interpreted with caution. Spillover from small countries in the region is likely to reflect aggregate shocks either to all emerging markets or to the region.

Figure 6.3. Selected Country Spreads and Latin American Emerging Markets Bond Index (EMBI) Spread, Pre- and Post-Uruguayan Crisis[1]
(In basis points)

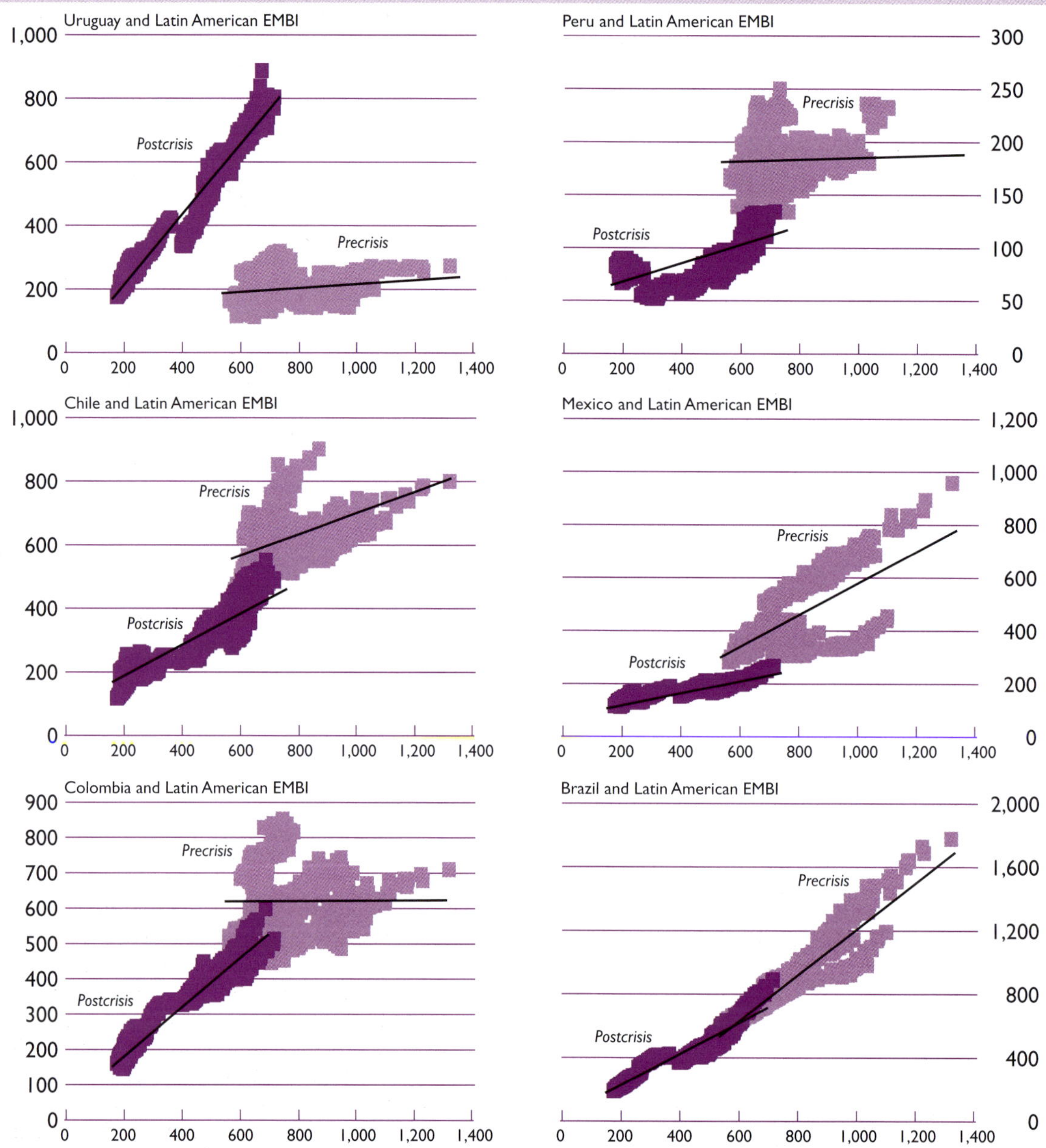

Sources: JPMorgan Chase & Co.; and República AFAP.
[1]Argentina is excluded, because most of Uruguay's postcrisis period coincides with the Argentine debt-restructuring process.

The heightened financial spillovers seem to be associated with the loss of investment grade. A simple comparison of sovereign spreads among Latin American countries reveals that during the late 1990s—when Uruguay had investment grade—spreads were significantly lower than those of most neighboring countries

Table 6.1. Sovereign Spread Correlation, Pre- and Postcrisis
(First differences)

Precrisis (January 1999–April 2002)	Argentina	Brazil	Chile	Colombia	EMBI	Latin America	Mexico	Peru	Uruguay
Argentina	1.00	0.32	0.02	0.13	0.28	0.31	0.23	0.19	0.08
Brazil		1.00	0.08	0.43	0.81	0.75	0.62	0.47	0.18
Chile			1.00	0.18	0.12	0.11	0.24	0.12	0.21
Colombia				1.00	0.42	0.36	0.47	0.32	0.26
EMBI					1.00	0.96	0.73	0.49	0.21
Latin America						1.00	0.55	0.40	0.18
Mexico							1.00	0.38	0.30
Peru								1.00	0.14
Uruguay									1.00
Argentina[1]	1.00	0.71	0.08	0.26	0.82	0.89	0.39	0.36	0.26
Postcrisis (June 2003–December 2006)									
Argentina	1.00	0.05	0.00	0.07	0.35	0.44	0.07	0.05	0.06
Brazil		1.00	0.21	0.67	0.82	0.86	0.59	0.63	0.55
Chile			1.00	0.24	0.28	0.25	0.33	0.23	0.14
Colombia				1.00	0.78	0.74	0.65	0.70	0.59
EMBI					1.00	0.95	0.75	0.69	0.63
Latin America						1.00	0.72	0.68	0.58
Mexico							1.00	0.61	0.51
Peru								1.00	0.52
Uruguay									1.00
Argentina[1]	1.00	0.62	0.06	0.53	0.69	0.72	0.50	0.45	0.36

Source: IMF staff calculations based on data from JPMorgan Chase & Co. and República AFAP.
[1]Excluding period between default and debt restructuring (Dec. 2001–May 2005).

and close to the ones of Chile—the other investment-grade economy in the region. Furthermore, Uruguayan spreads co-moved with those of Chile during that period. Since the 2002–03 crisis (and the associated loss of investment grade), however, Uruguayan spreads have moved close to those of other non-investment-grade economies (Figures 6.4 and 6.5).[7] Since then, Uruguay's credit rating has been recovering, but it is still below investment grade.[8]

[7]Increased correlation and financial spillovers from non-investment-grade countries may also reflect a change in the investor base for Uruguayan debt instruments because of the fact that some institutional investors (often with buy-and-hold strategies) are not allowed to hold instruments with speculative ratings.

[8]In June 2007, Standard & Poor's introduced a new methodology for rating sovereign debt issuers according to the expected recovery rate in the event of a default. Interestingly, Uruguay's recovery rating (2 = "substantial recovery") is higher than all graded countries in the region. A higher recovery rating combined with a lower overall rating—vis-à-vis neighboring countries—suggests that Uruguay's risk premium reflects mainly its vulnerability to external shocks rather than low "willingness to pay" (that is, Uruguay enjoys a good reputation for debt repayment).

What Drives Sovereign Spreads?

A vector error correction (VEC) model is estimated to quantify the contribution of external and domestic factors in driving Uruguay's sovereign spreads. The conclusions so far have followed from univariate analysis. However, the observed co-movement of spreads may reflect common global factors. A VEC model is estimated to control for these factors. This methodology, previously applied by Arora and Cerisola (2000) and Larzabal, Valdéz, and Laporta (2001), among others, also provides an adequate framework to disentangle short-term from long-term effects, while allowing for country-specific structural breaks.

The data set comprises monthly information for 1996–2006. Following the literature on determinants of sovereign spreads,[9] we choose public debt, the fis-

[9]For the most recent work in this topic, see Min (1998); Kamin and von Kleist (1999); Mauro, Sussman, and Yishay (2000); Garcia Herrero and Ortiz (2005); González Rozada and Levy Yeyati (2005); and Rojas and Jaque (2005).

Table 6.2. Pairwise Granger Causality Tests[1]

	Precrisis			Postcrisis		
Null Hypothesis	Number of observations	*F*-Statistic	Probability	Number of observations	*F*-Statistic	Probability
Uruguay does not Granger cause Brazil	828	1.12	0.327	896	0.90	0.407
Brazil does not Granger cause Uruguay		1.61	0.200		39.33	0.000***
Uruguay does not Granger cause Chile	726	2.56	0.078*	896	0.40	0.671
Chile does not Granger cause Uruguay		1.51	0.221		7.32	0.001***
Uruguay does not Granger cause Colombia	828	0.47	0.624	896	0.15	0.864
Colombia does not Granger cause Uruguay		0.28	0.757		25.23	0.000***
Uruguay does not Granger cause EMBI	828	0.96	0.384	896	0.06	0.944
EMBI does not Granger cause Uruguay		3.33	0.036**		28.23	0.000***
Uruguay does not Granger cause Latin America	828	0.93	0.396	896	0.39	0.680
Latin America does not Granger cause Uruguay		1.83	0.161		35.37	0.000***
Uruguay does not Granger cause Peru	828	0.93	0.396	896	1.40	0.247
Peru does not Granger cause Uruguay		1.21	0.300		19.45	0.000***
Uruguay does not Granger cause Mexico	828	1.15	0.316	896	0.40	0.672
Mexico does not Granger cause Uruguay		0.29	0.747		18.95	0.000***
Uruguay does not Granger cause Argentina	828	0.05	0.947	896	0.13	0.880
Argentina does not Granger cause Uruguay		6.11	0.002***		1.24	0.291
Uruguay does not Granger cause Argentina[2]	686	1.70	0.183	375	0.40	0.670
Argentina does not Granger cause Uruguay[2]		4.83	0.008***		8.62	0.000***

Source: IMF staff estimates.

Note: *, **, and *** represent significance at the 10 percent, 5 percent, and 1 percent level, respectively.

[1]Pairwise Granger causality test, for spreads first differences (2 lags). The pre- and postcrisis periods cover Jan. 1999–April 2002 and June 2003–December 2006, respectively.

[2]Excluding period of debt restructuring (December 2001–May 2005).

Figure 6.4. Standard & Poor's Credit Rating for Selected Latin American Countries, 1996–2006

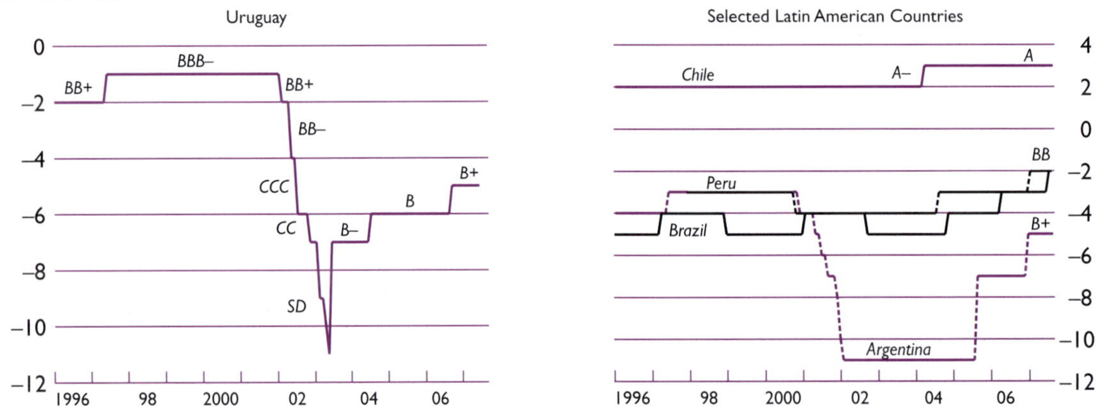

Source: Standard & Poor's.

Figure 6.5. Uruguay and Selected Latin American Country Spreads, Pre- and Postcrisis
(In basis points)

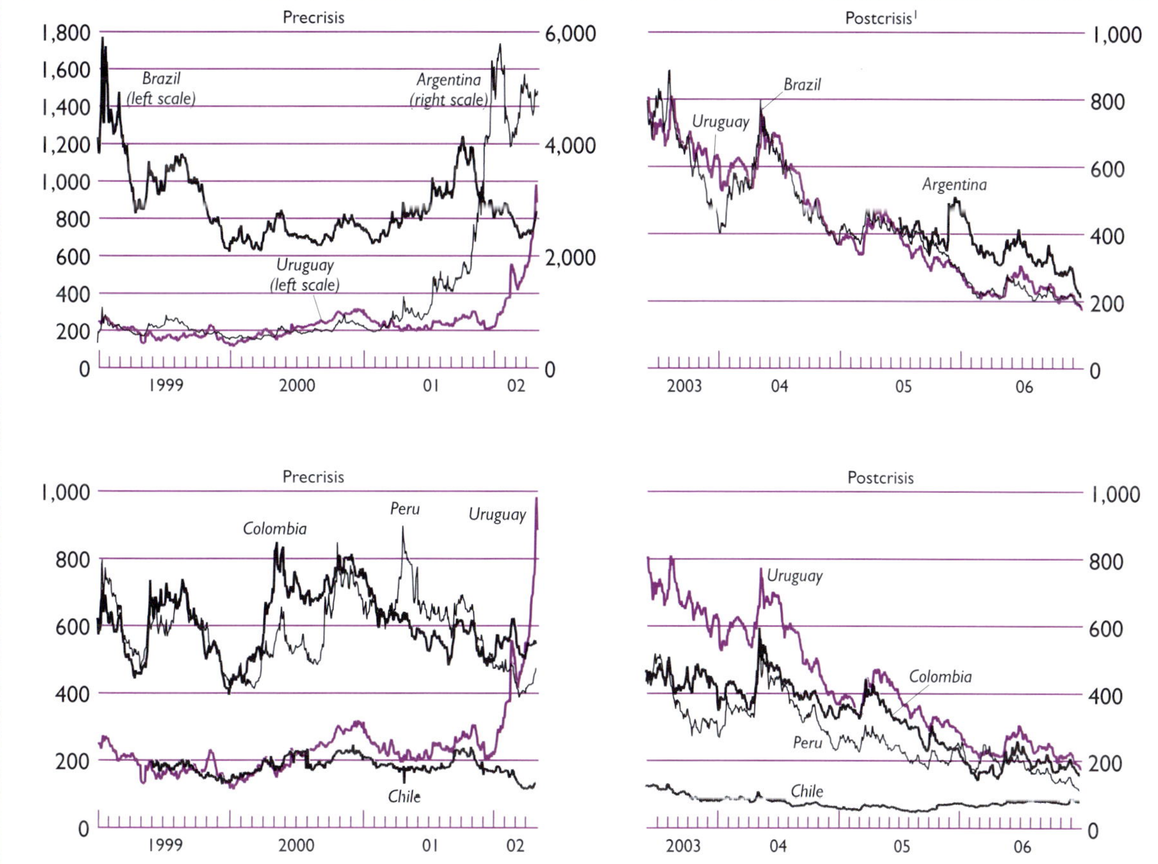

Sources: JPMorgan Chase & Co.; and República AFAP.
[1]Data for Argentine spreads are reported from July 2005 onward.

cal balance, and external debt (all as a share of GDP), reserve coverage (as a share of short-term debt and foreign currency deposits), and the real effective exchange rate to account for country fundamentals. These fundamentals reflect the economy's repayment capacity and its vulnerability to external shocks. To capture external factors, we use U.S. interest rates, terms of trade, the high-yield spread index, a market volatility measure (the Chicago Board Options Exchange Volatility Index, or VIX), and EMBI spreads. As a measure of sovereign risk, we use the Uruguayan Bond Index (UBI), instead of the EMBI, because of its longer time span.[10] Standard unit root tests (Augmented Dickey-Fuller) confirm that all variables are nonstationary, and support the notion of first-order integration (Table 6.3).

A cointegrating relationship is found among the Uruguayan spreads, public debt, reserve coverage, the terms of trade, the VIX, the high-yield index, and the Latin American EMBI.[11] From all variables considered that represent country fundamentals, only the public debt-to-GDP ratio and the reserve coverage are significant in the long-run relationship.[12] They both dis-

[10]The UBI is built from spreads of fixed-rate, dollar-denominated euronotes and global bonds issued by the Uruguayan government. UBI spreads are highly correlated with the Uruguayan EMBI spread produced by JPMorgan since the introduction of the latter in 1998.

[11]Both trace and maximum eigenvalue tests confirm the existence of a unique cointegrating relation.

[12]External debt is excluded because it is highly collinear with the public debt-to-GDP ratio.

Table 6.3. Unit Root Test: Augmented Dickey-Fuller (ADF)

	In Level		First Difference	
	t-Statistic	Probability[1]	*t*-Statistic	Probability[1]
PDGDP	–1.3836	0.5888	–2.8576	0.0531
RES	–0.0800	0.9600	–11.9500	0.0034
FBGDP	–1.5654	0.4985	–14.1541	0.0000
REER	–1.9292	0.3186	–16.3656	0.0000
USTBILL	–2.8390	0.0547	–3.7968	0.0035
HY	–1.2900	0.6300	–10.9300	0.0000
VIX	–3.1592	0.0240	–10.9867	0.0000
UBI	–2.4357	0.1337	–8.5676	0.0000
EMBI	–1.6415	0.4580	–10.8208	0.0000
EMBI_LA	–2.0950	0.2500	–8.3900	0.0000

Source: IMF staff estimates.

[1]MacKinnon (1996) one-sided *p*-values. Null hypothesis is unit root.

PDGDP Public debt as share of GDP (%)
RES Gross official reserves as share of short-term debt and foreign currency deposits
FBGDP Fiscal balance as percent of GDP
REER Real effective exchange rate
USTBILL U.S. treasury bill rate
HY Index of high-yield corporate spread (Merrill Lynch)
VIX Volatility index
EMBI JPMorgan Global EMBI spread
EMBI_LA JPMorgan Latin America EMBI spread

play the expected signs. In particular, a 1 percentage point increase in the public debt-to-GDP ratio increases the spread by about 17 bps, whereas a 1 percentage point increase in reserve coverage reduces the spread by about 28 bps (equation 1). Global factors, such as the terms of trade and the VIX, enter in the long-run relationship with the Uruguayan spread, and with the expected sign.[13] It is interesting to note that, in this specification without structural break, the effect of the Latin American EMBI spread on the Uruguayan spread is not significantly different from zero. As shown next, this reflects the presence of a structural break.

$$\underset{(339.35)}{UBI = 438.0} + \underset{(0.76)^{***}}{16.71PDGDP} - \underset{(3.18)^{***}}{27.6RES} - \underset{(3.36)^{**}}{8.73TOT} + \underset{(5.80)^{***}}{26.03VIX} + \underset{(0.16)}{0.02HY} - \underset{(0.15)}{0.13EMBI\_LA}. \quad (1)$$

If a structural break is allowed, the results confirm that the influence of other emerging market economies on Uruguay has increased following the loss of investment grade. Although the Latin American EMBI is not statistically significant by itself when included in the initial specification, evidence of financial spillover is found if a structural break associated with Uruguay's downgrading to speculative grade is allowed (equation 2). Moreover, estimates show that before the crisis (and after controlling for other global financial factors) the effect of regional shocks on Uruguayan spreads was negative, confirming the notion that Uruguay was perceived as a safe haven within the region.[14] After the loss of investment grade, however, the effect of regional shocks on the Uruguayan spread is positive. Similar, and even stronger, results are found if the global EMBI is used (equation 3). Although this may suggest that spillovers may stem from the emerging market asset class as a whole, it should be noted that Latin American countries (mainly Brazil and Mexico and previously Argentina) have a significant weight in the global index.

$$\underset{(312.36)}{UBI = 26.1} + \underset{(1.16)^{***}}{11.3PDGDP} - \underset{(3.52)^{***}}{15.6RES} - \underset{(3.00)^{**}}{6.81TOT} + \underset{(5.24)^{***}}{31.4VIX} + \underset{(0.16)^{**}}{0.37HY} - \underset{(0.14)^{**}}{0.33EMBI\_LA} + \underset{(0.09)^{***}}{0.49EMBI\_LA^{*}}(1 - Invgrade). \quad (2)$$

[13]Unlike previous work that has stressed the effect of U.S. interest rates on emerging market economy spreads, this link is not found for Uruguay.

[14]These results are consistent with previous work by Larzabal, Valdés, and Laporta (2001) covering the precrisis period that found that changes in the EMBI had a negative impact on Uruguayan spreads.

Table 6.4. Variance Decomposition[1]

Period	UBI	PDGDP	RES	TOT	VIX	HY	EMBI_LA	EMBI_LA* (1–INVGRADE)
1	72.30	2.31	3.38	1.30	11.76	0.15	2.07	6.73
2	52.91	7.24	3.60	2.20	20.30	0.05	2.28	11.42
3	39.12	10.42	4.40	3.28	25.31	0.05	2.58	14.84
4	30.73	12.07	5.06	4.41	27.85	0.09	2.83	16.95
5	25.85	12.89	5.52	5.53	28.91	0.15	3.04	18.10
6	22.98	13.34	5.83	6.56	29.23	0.19	3.20	18.68
7	21.21	13.61	6.03	7.48	29.21	0.21	3.31	18.94
8	20.03	13.80	6.17	8.29	29.07	0.21	3.40	19.04
9	19.16	13.95	6.27	8.98	28.90	0.22	3.45	19.07
10	18.47	14.07	6.36	9.57	28.75	0.22	3.49	19.06

Source: IMF staff estimates.

[1]Cholesky ordering: TOT VIX HY EMBI_LA EMBI_LA*(1–INVGRADE) PDGDP RES UBI.

$$UBI = \underset{(322.72)}{495.93} + \underset{(1.88)^{**}}{4.74}PDGDP - \underset{(3.54)^{***}}{18.8}RES - \underset{(3.07)^{*}}{5.65}TOT$$

$$+ \underset{(7.19)^{***}}{28.9}VIX + \underset{(0.15)}{0.25}HY - \underset{(0.13)^{***}}{0.49^{*}}EMBI$$

$$+ \underset{(0.18)^{***}}{1.14}EMBI^{*}(1 - Invgrade). \qquad (3)$$

Although fundamentals explain part of the variance of spreads, global factors have played an important role. Standard variance decomposition analysis identifies some 20 percent of the variance explained by country fundamentals and about 60 percent by external factors.[15] Among country fundamentals, public debt is most important in explaining Uruguay's spreads; among external factors, the VIX and the Latin American EMBI have the largest contributions (Table 6.4).

Conclusions

Although country fundamentals have explained part of the variation in sovereign spreads, external factors have played an important role. Moreover, external conditions have become more important following the 2002–03 crisis, and there is evidence of heightened financial spillover from other emerging market economies since then. Furthermore, econometric results suggest that, following the crisis, there has been a change in investors' perception of Uruguay's linkages with other emerging market economies. Such change seems to be associated with Uruguay's loss of investment grade during the crisis, as Uruguayan spreads have decoupled from those of Chile and moved closer to those of other non-investment-grade economies in the region.

These results suggest that, although Uruguay has made remarkable strides over the past years, it remains more exposed and vulnerable to global and regional shocks than it was before the crisis. In this context, continuing to strengthen the macroeconomic framework, diversifying trade destinations, further improving the public debt structure, and implementing pending structural reforms are key to regaining investment-grade status and, thus, insulating Uruguay from a possible deterioration in global conditions and from future regional shocks.

[15]Based on equation (2).

Bibliography

Arora, V., and M. Cerisola, 2000, "How Does U.S. Monetary Policy Influence Economic Conditions in Emerging Markets," IMF Working Paper 00/48 (Washington: International Monetary Fund).

Eble, S., 2006, *Uruguay's Growth History*, in *Uruguay: Selected Issues*, IMF Country Report No. 06/427 (Washington: International Monetary Fund).

Forbes, K., and R. Rigobon, 1999, "No Contagion, Only Interdependence: Measuring Stock Market Co-Movements," NBER Working Paper No. 7267 (Cambridge, Massachusetts: National Bureau of Economic Research).

Garcia Herrero, A., and A. Ortiz, 2005, "The Role of Global Risk Aversion in Explaining Latin American Sovereign Spreads," Working Paper No. 0505 (Madrid: Banco de España). Available via the Internet: www.bde.es/informes/be/docs/dt0505e.pdf.

Gelos, R.G., and R. Sahay, 2001, "Financial Market Spillovers in Transition Economies," *Economics of Transition*, Vol. 9 (March), pp. 53–86.

González Rozada, M., and E. Levy Yeyati, 2005, "Global Factors and Emerging Market Spreads," CIF Working

Paper No. 07/2005 (Buenos Aires: Universidad Torcuato Di Tella, Centro de Investigación en Finanzas). Available via the Internet: www.utdt.edu/Upload/CIF_wp/wpcif–072005.pdf.

Kamin, S., and Karsten von Kleist, 1999, "*The Evolution and Determinants of Emerging Market Credit Spreads in the 1990s*," International Finance Discussion Paper No. 653 (Washington: Federal Reserve Board of Governors). Available via the Internet: www.federalreserve.gov/pubs/ifdp/1999/653/ifdp653.pdf.

Kanagasabapathy, K., and Rajan Goyal, 2002, "Yield Spread as a Leading Indicator of Real Economic Activity: An Empirical Exercise on the Indian Economy," IMF Working Paper 02/91 (Washington: International Monetary Fund).

Larzabal, M., M. Valdés, and S. Laporta, 2001, "Spread Soberano: Evidencia Empírica del Caso Uruguayo" (Montevideo: Central Bank of Uruguay, Departamento de Estudios de República AFAP).

Mauro, P., N. Sussman, and Y. Yishay, 2000, "Emerging Market Spreads: Then Versus Now," IMF Working Paper 00/190 (Washington: International Monetary Fund).

Min, H., 1998, "Determinants of Emerging Market Bond Spread: Do Economic Fundamentals Matter?" Policy Research Working Paper No. 1899 (Washington: World Bank).

Rojas, A., and F. Jaque, 2003, "Determinants of the Chilean Sovereign Spread: Is It Purely Fundamentals?" *Money Affairs*, Vol. 16 (July–December).

Part 3

Financial Vulnerabilities and Insurance Mechanisms

VII Has the Uruguayan Financial System Become More Resilient to Shocks? An Analysis Adapting the Merton Framework to a Country Without Equity Market Data

Marcos Rietti Souto

Following substantial restructuring and enhanced supervision in the aftermath of the 2002 crisis, financial sector soundness indicators in Uruguay have strengthened considerably. The Uruguayan banking system is now profitable and has become better capitalized. It is also highly liquid, although this partly reflects a sharp reduction in lending. Nonperforming loans have fallen to 2 percent of total loans (excluding the housing bank), and nonresident deposits, which proved volatile in the face of negative external developments, are well below precrisis levels. In addition, the regulation and supervision of the financial system have improved significantly. However, despite low short-term risks, important medium-term vulnerabilities remain, particularly stemming from high dollarization (see also IMF, 2006).

This chapter assesses the extent of remaining vulnerabilities of the banking sector using a variant of the Merton (1973 and 1974) framework. To this end, the study constructs a set of credit risk indicators, which are then used to compare banks' risk profile at the time of the 2002 banking crisis with today's conditions and examines the impact of potential shocks on the various risk indicators. In contrast to the Merton framework, which uses market data to capture the collective views and expectations of market participants, this chapter uses book value data from balance sheets because of the absence of market data in Uruguay. The approach still incorporates volatility into the estimations, a key feature of the Merton framework for capturing nonlinearities in the credit risk indicators, especially during periods of distress.

Despite simplifying assumptions, the methodology captures well several stylized facts of the 2002 banking crisis and suggests that the system has become more resilient to shocks. In particular, it identifies, as early as the first quarter of 2002, a deterioration in the credit risk indicators of the banking sector. When the methodology is applied to the corporate sector, significant distress events can be perceived toward the last quarter of 2002. The methodology also points to a substantial improvement in the credit risk indicators since the 2002 crisis, in line with the restructuring process pursued over the past years. Consistent with the conclusions of the stress tests of the IMF's 2006 Financial Sector Assessment Program (FSAP) and the 2007 update prepared by the authorities, this study shows that, notwithstanding remaining vulnerabilities, banks have become more resilient to shocks. Thus, the methodology used in this chapter appears to have the potential to be a useful tool kit for economies that lack (or have shallow) equity markets.

This chapter first briefly describes the Merton framework, then presents the more "traditional" stress tests conducted during the 2006 FSAP mission and updated by the authorities in 2007 to assess whether the banking system has become more resilient since the 2006 FSAP exercise. The chapter then estimates credit risk indicators using the modified Merton framework; also, with information on total assets and liabilities from the stress tests, this section simulates shocks to these indicators.

Merton Framework

The Merton framework offers clear advantages over traditional vulnerability analyses, including by incorporating volatility explicitly into the estimations.[1] The approach relies on observable market information on the value and volatility of liabilities (and equity) to derive the value of nonobservable quantities, such as the asset value and asset volatility. This information is then combined to estimate risk indicators, such as the distance to distress (a measure of how far a firm is from defaulting),

[1]See Gapen and others (2004 and 2005) and Jones and Gray (2006) for examples of application of the Merton framework to government, banking, and corporate sectors' balance sheets.

Figure 7.1. Merton Framework

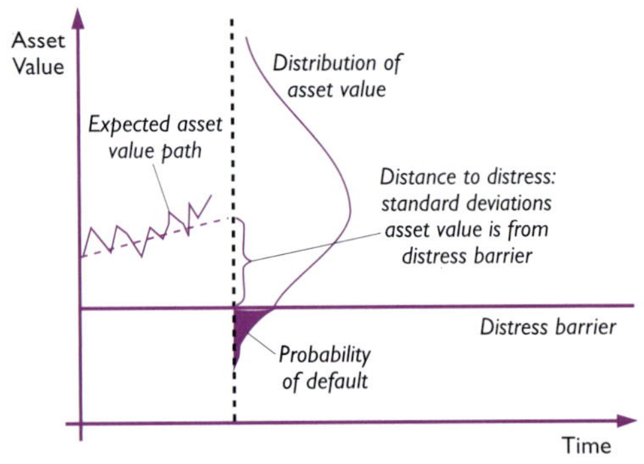

Source: Merton (1973).

default probability, credit spread, and expected losses given a default. In contrast to more traditional vulnerability analyses, this framework incorporates market volatility when estimating credit risk. Volatility is crucial in capturing nonlinear changes in risk, especially during times of stress when small shocks can gain momentum and trigger systemic repercussions.

The basic idea is to model a firm's equity as a (junior) contingent claim on the residual value of its assets. In the event of default, all the firm's assets are used to pay the senior stakeholders (for example, debt holders); otherwise, equity holders receive the difference between the value of assets and debt. Thus, the equity of the firm can be seen as a call option on the residual value of the firm's assets (Figure 7.1). This framework enables a rich characterization of a firm's (or sovereign's) balance sheet and the derivation of several credit risk indicators (for example, distance to distress, default probability, and credit spreads).

With information on the market value and volatility of equity and the value of debt, it is possible to estimate the implied value for assets and volatility, through the Black and Scholes option formula. Firms are assumed to default whenever the value of assets falls below a given "distress" barrier. It is then possible to estimate a set of credit risk indicators, including distance to distress, default probability, credit spread, and expected losses in the event of default.[2]

Given the lack of an equity market in Uruguay, this study incorporates volatility into the estimation of credit risk indicators by using book value data. Although this reduces to some extent its forward-looking nature, the approach still retains key characteristics, such as proper analysis of asset volatility. Moreover, balance sheet data appear to capture well changes in the financial health of Uruguayan banks during the sample period, without particularly long lags.

Stress Tests

This section summarizes the main results of stress tests conducted by the 2006 FSAP and updated by the authorities in 2007.

2006 FSAP Stress Tests

The 2006 FSAP stress tests focused on the impact of shocks on banks' capital adequacy ratio (CAR) and liquidity ratio.[3] The institutions included all private banks, cooperatives, finance companies, offshore banks, and the state-owned Banco de la República Oriental del Uruguay (BROU); these institutions represented 80 percent of the financial system assets. The stress tests were performed on exposures, on a bank-by-bank basis, as of June 2005 (main assumptions are listed in Table 7.1). They included sensitivity analysis with respect to the interest rate, exchange rate, and credit risk, as well as macroeconomic scenarios involving a domestic supply shock (severe weather conditions), a current account shock (corresponding to a drop in Argentine GDP of 10 percent), and a capital account shock (corresponding to a rise in the three-month LIBOR to 7 percent per year).

The 2006 results indicated that banks had improved considerably but remained vulnerable to severe shocks. Following these large shocks, several institutions would be undercapitalized or their CAR would fall below the minimum required capital ratio, particularly under the capital account shock scenario. However, banks appeared to be resilient to moderate fluctuations in the exchange rate, interest rate, liquidity, and credit reclassification, with only a few institutions having their CAR fall below the minimum required capital ratio.

Stress Test Update

The 2007 update of the stress tests indicates that banks are more resilient to economic shocks. The exercise was updated using December 2006 data for the shocks that yielded the worst results in the 2006 FSAP. The current account shock results in a drop of the average CAR of 4 percent in the update, against 8 percent in the 2006 FSAP; the capital account shock yields a drop of 10 per-

[2]Technical details are provided in Appendix 7.1.

[3]For more details on the stress tests' assumptions, see IMF (2006).

Table 7.1. 2006 Financial Sector Assessment Program: Stress Tests Assumption
(In percent)

Risk Factor	Current Account Shock	Capital Account Shock
Δ Real exchange rate	5	12
Δ Argentina private consumption	−10	−10
Δ Argentina nominal exchange rate	45	45
Δ Argentina real exchange rate	30	30
Δ Foreign prices	–5	−13
Δ Domestic prices	7	15
Δ Nominal exchange rate	17	48
Δ GDP[1]	–4	–8
Country risk[2]	500 to 550 bps	> 600 bps

Source: IMF staff calculations.
[1]GDP gap where long-term GDP growth is equal to 3 percent.
[2]The country risk was calibrated according to similar historical episodes.

Figure 7.2. Liquidity Ratios After Stress Shocks
(In percent)

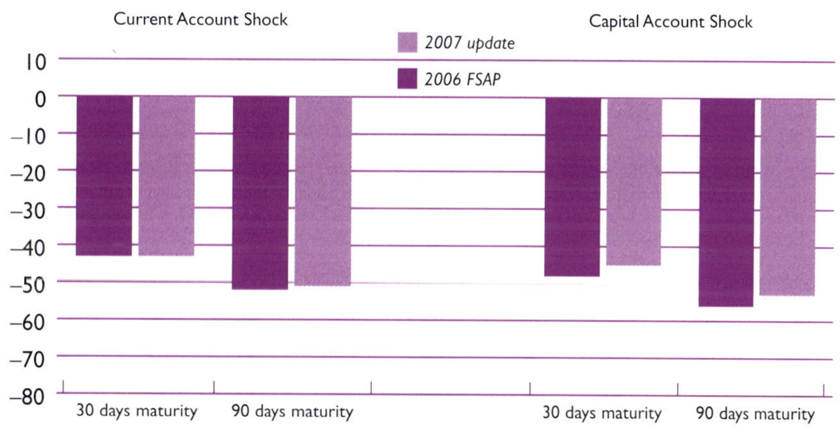

Source: Central Bank of Uruguay staff calculations.
Note: FSAP is the Financial Sector Assessment Program (IMF).

cent, against 22 percent in the 2006 FSAP (Figure 7.2). Liquidity ratios dropped modestly in the 2007 update, compared with the 2006 FSAP exercise. Under the current account shock scenario, liquidity ratios for assets and liabilities maturing in 30 days or fewer were, on average, 43 percent in both the 2006 FSAP and 2007 update; under the capital account shock scenario, these ratios fell, on average, 48 percent in the 2006 FSAP and 45 percent in the 2007 update. Similar drops in liquidity ratios are observed for assets and liabilities maturing in 90 days or fewer (Figure 7.3).

Modified Merton Framework

This section uses the modified Merton framework to assess whether the estimated credit risk indicators capture well the main stylized facts of the 2002 banking crisis and the ensuing recovery. Also, the framework is used to estimate the impact of current and capital account shocks, replicating those defined in the stress tests, in an effort to incorporate volatility as an additional dimension to these tests, which rely only on asset and liability levels.

Figure 7.3. Capital Adequacy Ratio (Percentage of Risk-Weighted Assets) After Stress Shocks

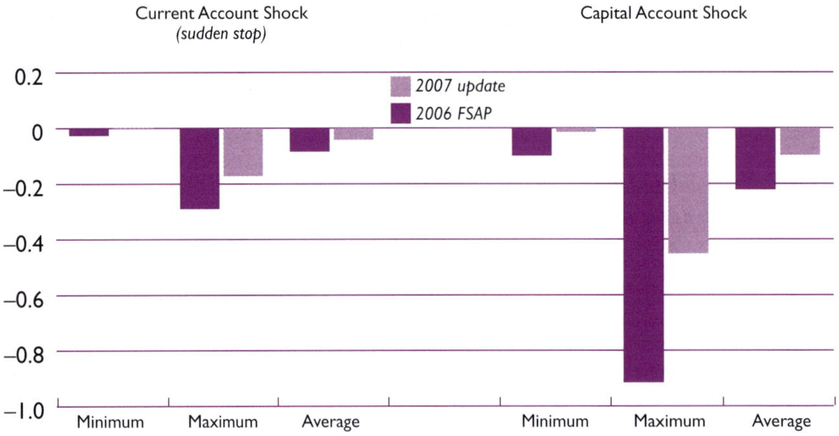

Source: Central Bank of Uruguay staff calculations.
Note: FSAP is the Financial Sector Assessment Program (IMF).

Estimating Risk Indicators

To estimate credit risk indicators, it is key to adjust balance sheet data to reflect underlying values and volatilities better.[4] First, beyond the deterioration in assets reflected through provisions, the data were adjusted by the expected losses arising from companies facing the same shocks. Second, the data were adjusted to take into account the liquidity/capital support provided during the 2002 crisis (US$2.4 billion, see Table 7.2), which was masking the decrease in total asset value and volatility in the published financial statements (see Appendix 7.1 for details).

The expected losses from the corporate sector were estimated using the modified Merton framework. Despite the limitations of the methodology (see Appendix 7.1 for technical details), the results appear to be in line with the stylized facts: in 2002, there was an increase in expected losses from companies that defaulted, owing in part to a higher volatility of total assets; in subsequent years, once the volatility of assets declined and the balance sheet accounts improved, expected losses returned to the precrisis levels (Figure 7.4).[5]

The adjusted book value data for 12 banks were used to estimate time series for credit risk indicators for the banking sector.[6] With the adjusted set of assets and asset volatilities, a time series of default probabilities for each individual bank was estimated—with the default probability of the banking sector estimated by applying, to the individual default probabilities, a weighted average (based on each bank's proportion of total assets).

The indicator for the expected default probability (EDP) of the banking system estimated through the modified Merton framework appears to be sensible (Figure 7.5). The framework predicts near-zero one-year default probabilities (with volatility measured over total assets) prior to the 2002 crisis; this suggests that the 2002 shock was largely unanticipated. However, starting in March 2002, the estimated EDP starts to increase, reaching 45 percent in September 2002. Since then, the default probability has declined substantially, to near zero again by end-2006. This is consistent with a reduction in asset volatility and the substantial "clean-up" in banks' portfolios associated with the restructuring process.

Using the Modified Merton Framework

Simulating the impact of potential shocks on the estimated default probability using the modified Mer-

[4]A capital injection to the banking system, for example, would mask the real volatility in the assets being depleted to meet the deposit withdrawals from a deposit run.

[5]The sample of firms used to construct a time series on total assets and estimate their volatility is taken from de Brun and others (2006) and covers the period 1995–2005.

[6]Twelve banks covering 70 percent of the system are BROU, Banco A.C.A.C., Discount Bank, Santander, Frances Bank, HSBC, Surinvest, Citibank, ABN Amro Bank, BankBoston, Lloyds Bank, and Banco de La Nacion Argentina. Quarterly balance sheet data are available for 2000–01 and monthly data for January 2002 to December 2006.

Table 7.2. Total Government Assistance to Banks[1]
(In millions of U.S. dollars, as of August 2002)

	Total	Public Banks	Private Banks
Total assistance	2,417	1,228	1,189
Of which: in pesos	33	10	23
Capitalization	33	0	33
Central bank	563	258	305
Article 36/37	391	258	133
Overdraft	173	0	173
FFSB (Jun. 2002)	449	0	449
FSBS (Aug. 2002)	1,373	970	403

Source: Seelig (2006).
Note: FFSB is Fondo de Fortalecimiento del Sistema Bancario. FSBS is the Fund for the Stabilization of the Banking System.
[1]Includes assistance in pesos, evaluated at Ur$28.8/US$1.

Figure 7.4. Expected Losses Given Default in the Corporate Sector
(In millions of U.S. dollars)

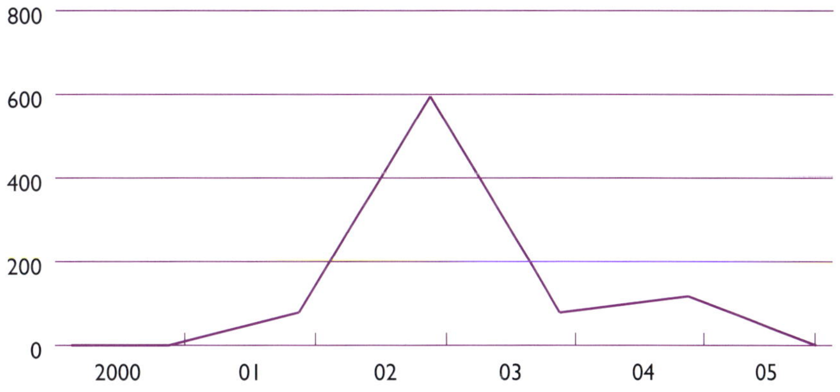

Source: IMF staff estimates.

ton framework provides a basis to assess the solidity of the improved risk indicators beyond the traditional stress tests. In particular, the estimated near-zero probability of default is to a large extent the result of the currently low volatility environment, given that volatility is an important parameter in the estimation of the EDP. Because standard stress tests provide information only on banks' levels of assets and liabilities following shocks, this chapter simulates asset volatilities, consistent with the after-shock level of assets for each bank (Figure 7.6).

Results from a simulation of a scenario like the 2002 crisis show that banks have become significantly more resilient to macroeconomic shocks, further confirming the thrust of the FSAP's stress tests results (Figure 7.7).[7] Using the FSAP's severe capital and current account shocks, the default probabilities reach 24 percent and 14 percent, respectively—far below the 45 percent default probability predicted by the model for the peak

[7]This is not surprising given that the results from the stress tests are used to shock the modified Merton framework.

Figure 7.5. Banking Sector Default Probability
(In percent)

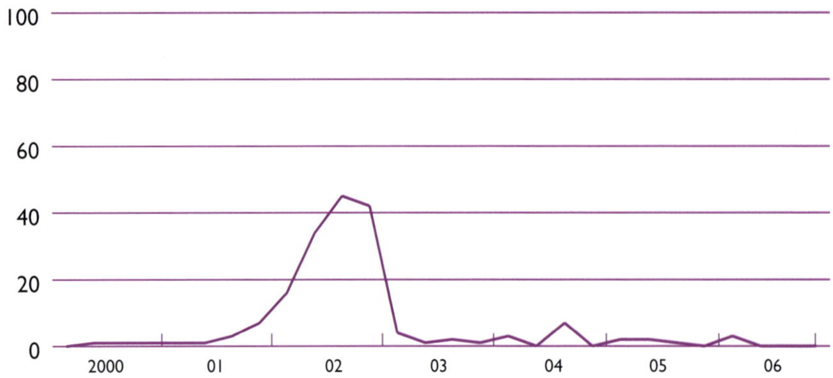

Source: IMF staff estimates.

Figure 7.6. Relationship Between Assets and Asset Volatility in Uruguay

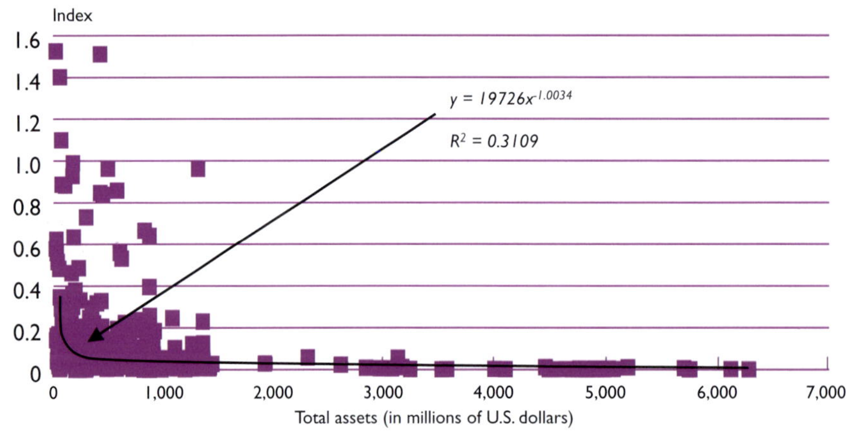

Source: IMF staff estimates.

of the 2002 crisis. However, default probabilities under a 2002-crisis-like stress scenario remain significant, thus underscoring the need to reduce vulnerabilities in the banking system further.

Conclusions

A modified Merton framework, applied to the case of the Uruguayan banking system, appears to be promising for countries without equity markets. Although the methodology is based on balance sheet information, and not on market valuations, the estimated asset volatility and default probability time series seem quite sensible. In particular, they track well the deterioration of the system during the 2002 crisis, including through plausible numerical point estimates for default probability. In addition, the framework proves useful to simulate the effects of possible changes in macroeconomic conditions to individual banks. The latter improves on

Figure 7.7. Default Probabilities: A Scenario Analysis
(In percent)

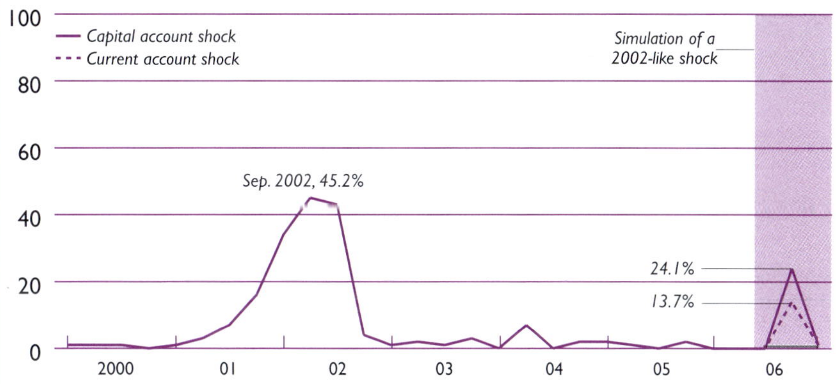

Source: IMF staff estimates.

conventional portfolio stress tests that rely only on asset and liability levels by explicitly incorporating volatility into the analysis.

The analysis suggests that, although still important, vulnerabilities have continued to decline, further confirming the FSAP stress tests results. The estimated default probability reaches only half the level measured at the peak of the 2002 crisis, even under a substantial shock in the capital account. The impact of a shock in the current account is even smaller. The results also show, however, that vulnerabilities remain, suggesting that sustained efforts to reduce them further over the medium term are necessary.

Appendix 7.1. Estimating Risk Indicators for the Corporate and Banking Sectors

Estimating Corporate Sector Expected Losses

The main challenge consists in generating a consistent time series on total assets to estimate volatilities on total asset returns. This challenge arises because the sample size (number of firms) in the data set changes over time. An estimate of total assets as the sum across all firms at each point may capture variations in total assets that are simply results of changes in the data set sample. To control for this fact, Mitton (2006) suggests estimating the following panel regression for the average firm within the firm:

$$Total\ Assets_{it} = \alpha + Firm_i + \beta \cdot Year_t + \varepsilon_{it}, \qquad \text{(A.1)}$$

where $Firm_i$ represents firm-fixed effects and $Year_t$ represents a full set of year-specific dummy variables. The time series on the total assets is then constructed as[8]

$$Total\ Assets_t = \hat{\alpha} + \hat{\beta}_t. \qquad \text{(A.2)}$$

This estimate provides a complete time series for (annual) total assets covering the period 1994–2006, which makes it possible to estimate returns as continuously compounded, that is, $r_t = \ln(TA_t/TA_{t-1})$. To estimate volatilities, it is then possible to use an exponentially weighted moving average (EWMA):

$$\sigma_t^2 = r_t^2, \text{ for } t = 1994, \qquad \text{(A.3)}$$

$$\sigma_t^2 = (1-\lambda)r_t^2 + \lambda\sigma_{t-1}^2, \text{ for } t = 1995, 1996, \ldots 2006, \qquad \text{(A.4)}$$

where r_t is the return on the total assets at time t, λ is the decay factor (we are using $\lambda = 0.95$, following common practice), and σ_t^2 is the volatility at time t.

It is instructive to express the distance to distress in another (approximated) way:

$$D2D = \frac{TA - DB}{TA \times \sigma_{TA}} = \frac{\frac{TA - DB}{TA}}{\sigma_{TA}}, \qquad \text{(A.5)}$$

[8]There are also missing observations for 2002 and 2006. To obtain the value for 2002, the average values for total assets for 2000, 2001, 2003, and 2004 are used. To obtain the value for 2006, the average growth on total assets from 2003 to 2005 is used.

Figure 7A.1. Uruguay's Corporate Sector: Components of Distance to Distress

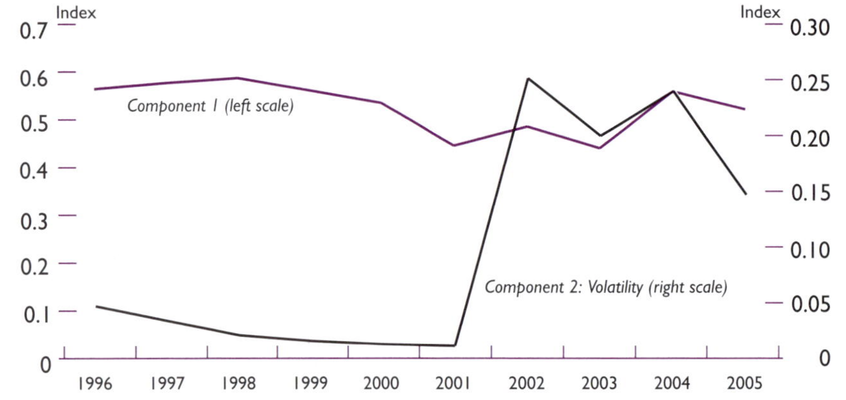

Source: IMF staff estimates.

where *TA* is the total assets, *DB* is the distress barrier, and σ_{TA} is the volatility of total assets. The numerator of equation (A.5) is the component 1, which represents the distance of total assets to the distress barrier, as a fraction of total assets (how far from distress). The denominator, σ_{TA}, is the component 2. Appendix Figure 7A.1 depicts the evolution of the distance-to-distress components for the corporate sector.

It is clear that (1) volatility increased substantially in 2002, consistent with the banking crisis that led to a depreciation of the peso, adversely affecting companies with a substantial exposure to foreign exchange rate risk; (2) after 2002, volatility declined, but still remained above precrisis levels; and (3) component 1, $(TA-DB)/TA$, started to decline in 1999, reaching its lowest levels in 2001–03 and showing rising balance sheet mismatches in the corporate sector. Component 1 improved slightly in 2004, but it still remained below precrisis levels.

With information on assets, asset volatility, interest rates, and liabilities, it is possible to obtain the expected losses, given default (Merton, 1977):

$$P = Be^{-rt} N(-d_2) - AN(-d_1), \qquad \text{(A.6)}$$

where *P* represents the expected losses, *B* represents the distress barrier, *r* is the risk-free interest rate, *t* is the maturity (for the sake of simplicity, we are looking into one-year-ahead measures), *A* is the total asset, and d_1 and d_2 are known parameters in the Black and Scholes formula.[9]

Estimating Banking Sector Default Probability

To estimate volatility for banks' total assets, it is first necessary to construct a time series of return on assets as $r_t = \ln(TA_t/TA_{t-1})$. Then, as for the corporate sector, volatilities are estimated using the EWMA updating expressions:[10]

$$\sigma_t^2 = r_t^2, \text{ for } t = \text{2000Q1 or 2002M1 and} \qquad \text{(A.7)}$$

$$\sigma_t^2 = (1-\lambda)r_t^2 + \lambda\sigma_{t-1}^2, \text{ for t} = \text{2000Q2}, \ldots, \text{2001Q4 or 2002M2}, \ldots, \text{2006M12}. \qquad \text{(A.8)}$$

It is also possible to estimate volatilities using time series on return on deposits. Given that changes in deposits may be viewed as a measure of customer's confidence in the bank, it may be a better proxy for "market-related" volatility. We use both sets of volatility to estimate risk indicators. Both approaches yielded similar results.

The liquidity shock hitting the banking sector in 2002 is captured in Appendix Figure 7A.2. Liquid assets were drained at a fast pace in an effort to meet the increasing deposit withdrawals that followed the Argentine crisis. Following this event, volatilities remained at low levels, reflecting the restructuring of the banking sector. The second hump in deposit volatilities reveals a second run by depositors that took place early in 2003.

Once asset volatility has been estimated, it is then possible to estimate distance to distress and default

[9]See Hull (2000) for the precise formulas and definition.

[10]For banks, we also use $\lambda = 0.95$.

Figure 7A.2. Uruguay's Banking Sector Volatilities

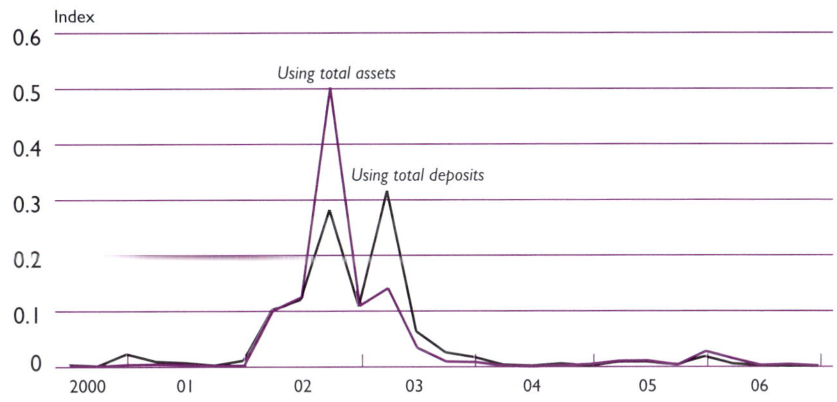

Source: IMF staff estimates.

probability for each bank individually.[11] Risk indicators for the banking sector can be obtained as weighted averages of individual banks, weighted by banks' total assets.

Bibliography

de Brun, J., N. Gandelman, H. Kamil, and A. C. Porzecanski, 2006, "The Fixed-Income Market in Uruguay" (unpublished; Montevideo: Universidad ORT Uruguay).

Dwyer, D.W., G. Guo, and F. Hood III, 2006, "Moody's KMV RISKCALC™ V3.1 US Banks: Modeling Methodology" (San Francisco: Moody's/KMV).

Gapen, Michael T., Dale F. Gray, Cheng Hoon Lim, and Yingbin Xiao, 2005, "Measuring and Analyzing Sovereign Risk with Contingent Claims," IMF Working Paper 05/155 (Washington: International Monetary Fund). Available via the Internet: www.imf.org/external/pubs/ft/wp/2005/wp05155.pdf.

Gapen, Michael T., Dale F. Gray, Yingbin Xiao, and Cheng Hoon Lim, 2004, "The Contingent Claims Approach to Corporate Vulnerability Analysis: Estimating Default Risk and Economy-Wide Risk Transfer," IMF Working Paper 04/121 (Washington: International Monetary Fund). Available via the Internet: www.imf.org/external/pubs/ft/wp/2004/wp04121.pdf.

Gray, D.F., R.C. Merton and Z. Bodie, 2006, "A New Framework for Analyzing and Managing Macrofinancial Risks of an Economy," NBER Working Paper No. 12637 (Cambridge, Massachusetts: National Bureau for Economic Research).

Hull, J.C., 2000, *Options, Futures, and Other Derivatives* (Upper Saddle River, New Jersey: Prentice Hall).

International Monetary Fund, *International Financial Statistics* (various issues).

———, 2006, "Stress Testing the Banking Sector," Box 2 in *Uruguay: Financial System Stability Assessment*, IMF Country Report No. 06/439 (Washington).

Jones, Matthew T., and Dale F. Gray, 2006, "Measuring Sovereign and Banking Sector Risk in Indonesia: An Application of the Contingent Claims Approach," in *Indonesia, Selected Issues Papers*, IMF Country Report No. 06/318 (Washington: International Monetary Fund).

Merton, Robert C., 1973, "Theory of Rational Option Pricing," *Bell Journal of Economics and Management Science*, Vol. 4 (Spring), pp. 141–83.

———, 1974, "On the Pricing of Corporate Debt: The Risk Structure of Interest Rates," *Journal of Finance*, Vol. 29 (May), pp. 449–70.

———, 1977, "An Analytic Derivation of the Cost of Deposit Insurance and Loan Guarantees: An Application of Modern Option Pricing Theory," *Journal of Banking and Finance*, Vol. 1 (June), pp. 3–11.

Mitton, T., 2006, "Why Have Debt Ratios Increased for Firms in Emerging Markets?" (unpublished; Provo, Utah: Brigham Young University).

Seelig, S., 2006, "Resolving the Banking Crisis in Uruguay" (unpublished; Washington: International Monetary Fund).

[11]See Gapen and others (2004 and 2005) for details on the formulas.

VIII Optimal Level of Reserves in Financially Dollarized Economies: The Case of Uruguay

Fernando M. Gonçalves

The recent increase in holdings of foreign reserves in many countries has renewed the interest in assessing the motives and adequacy of reserve accumulation. Because reserves provide protection against external shocks but are costly to carry, a careful assessment of the adequacy of reserve levels is warranted.

One frequently cited motive for holding large amounts of foreign reserves is to self-insure against costly crises.[1] Reserves can be useful for mitigating the fall in domestic consumption that may result from a sudden stop of external credit and/or a run on banks' foreign currency deposits. This insurance role of reserves is more pronounced in dollarized economies, where financial account reversals and bank runs typically have larger adverse effects because of currency mismatches in the balance sheets of economic agents.[2]

Foreign reserves played a significant role in mitigating the effects of the 2002 crisis in Uruguay. Following the Argentine crisis in 2001, Uruguay experienced a sudden stop of external credit and a banking crisis.[3] Figure 8.1 shows the resulting large financial account reversal and withdrawal of dollar deposits. It also depicts the large amount of reserves—a significant part of which was made available through an IMF arrangement—used to offset the outflows. Although output dropped significantly, the use of reserves helped offset a potentially much larger fall in economic activity.

This chapter assesses the adequacy of foreign reserves in Uruguay from a prudential perspective. The framework derived by Jeanne and Rancière (2006; henceforth, JR) is extended to incorporate the dollarization of bank deposits explicitly. The chapter illustrates the relevance of this extension by calibrating the model for Uruguay, a highly dollarized country in which higher reserve levels are valuable for prudential reasons, even though short-term foreign currency debt is low.

Vulnerabilities and the Role of Reserves in Uruguay

Short-term foreign currency debt is now at historically low levels.[4] Whereas in 2002 short-term foreign currency indebtedness of public and private sectors combined was more than 40 percent of GDP, by end-2006 it had fallen to less than 3 percent of GDP (Figure 8.2).

Despite significant progress, high deposit dollarization and nonresidents' deposits remain sources of vulnerability. As illustrated by the 2002 crisis experience, nonresidents' deposits are more susceptible to large withdrawals than are residents' deposits (Figure 8.3). In recent years, nonresidents' foreign currency deposits have decreased sharply, reaching 9 percent of GDP at end-2006, thus representing a significant reduction in banking sector vulnerability. Nonetheless, foreign currency deposits remained at the high level of about 37 percent of GDP in end-2006. Thus, although risks have been reduced considerably since the crisis, Uruguay's dollarization of deposits remains one of the highest in the world and a major vulnerability for the Uruguayan economy.

Reserve adequacy measures should take into account the degree of deposit dollarization. Traditional measures would suggest that Uruguay holds comfortable reserve levels (Figure 8.4).[5] Reserves are now well above all short-term foreign currency debt (Guidotti-Greenspan rule), in contrast to the years prior to the 2002 crisis. Also, coverage of imports has consistently exceeded three months, except in

---

[1]Countries may accumulate reserves to achieve a range of objectives not restricted to self-insurance. Other possibilities include (1) making exchange rate markets more efficient by providing liquidity when needed; (2) limiting exchange rate volatility ("leaning against the wind"); and (3) pursuing, even if temporarily, export-led growth supported by a de facto fixed exchange rate (see European Central Bank, 2006; and Becker and others, 2007).

[2]For an analysis of balance sheet mismatches in Uruguay, see Kamil (2006).

[3]See de la Plaza and Sirtaine (2005) for a detailed analysis of the 2002 crisis in Uruguay.

[4]The definition of public and private short-term debt is in a remaining maturity basis. Public sector short-term foreign currency debt includes both domestic and external debt.

[5]See Wijnholds and Kapteyn (2001) for a discussion of traditional benchmark measures of reserve adequacy.

Figure 8.1. Financial Account Reversal, Dollar Deposits, and Reserves in Uruguay
(In percent of 2001 GDP)

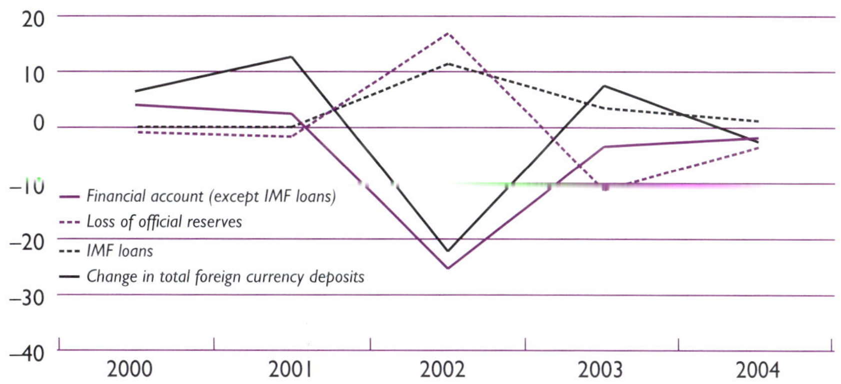

Sources: IMF staff calculations; and Central Bank of Uruguay.

Figure 8.2. Short-Term Foreign Currency Debt and Foreign Currency Deposits in Uruguay
(In percent of GDP)

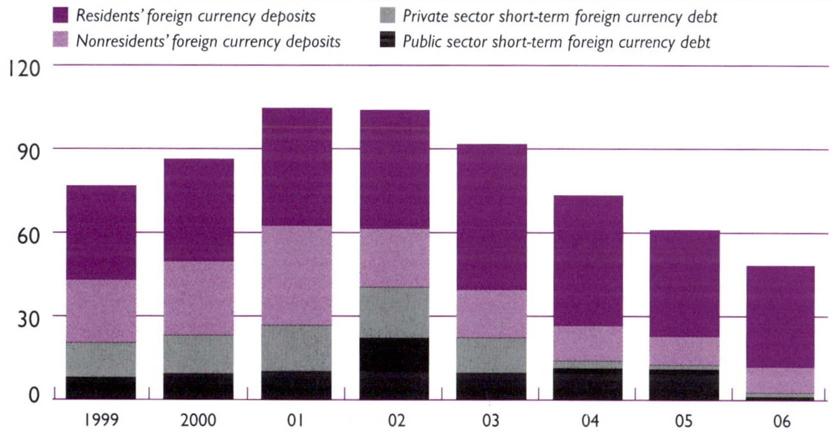

Source: Central Bank of Uruguay.

the year of the crisis. The Uruguayan economy was particularly vulnerable to a bank run prior to the 2002 crisis: reserves covered only 18 percent of dollar deposits. Reserve coverage of dollar deposits has increased substantially since then to about 35 percent (more than 100 percent of nonresidents' deposits). However, further analysis is needed to establish whether reserves now provide an appropriate balance between costs and protection against a major withdrawal of dollar deposits.

Figure 8.3. Withdrawal of Foreign Currency Deposits in 2002
(In percent of 2001 GDP)

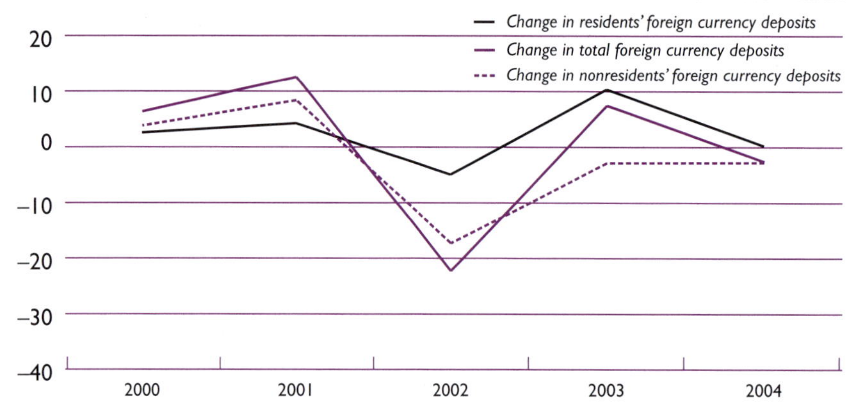

Source: Central Bank of Uruguay.

Figure 8.4. Benchmark Measures of Reserve Adequacy

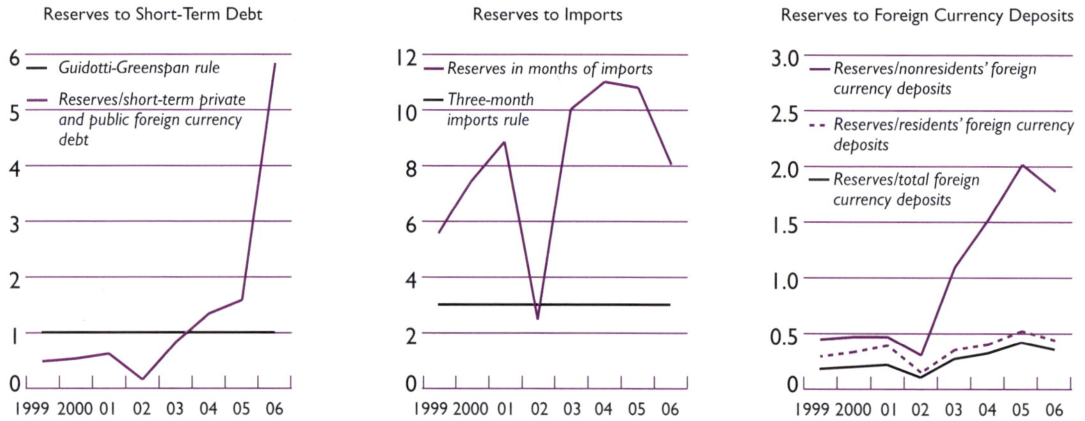

Sources: IMF, *International Financial Statistics*; Central Bank of Uruguay; and authors' calculations.

Optimal Level of Reserves

What is the optimal level of foreign reserves for self-insurance purposes in a financially dollarized economy? To address this question, the JR model is extended to take into account dollar-denominated deposits explicitly. The resulting expression for the optimal level of reserves is shown in equation (1) (a full derivation of the model is in Appendix 8.1). It includes parameters computed from actual data (Table 8.1) and also parameters that need to be calibrated and are assumed fixed during the sample period (Table 8.2).

The formula balances the consumption-smoothing benefits with the quasi-fiscal costs of holding reserves. It states that optimal reserves are increas-

Table 8.1. Variable Parameters
(In percent)

	1999	2000	2001	2002	2003	2004	2005	2006
Public sector short-term foreign currency debt/GDP (λ_G)	8.1	9.4	10.2	22.2	9.7	11.3	11.1	1.3
Private sector short-term foreign currency debt/GDP (λ_P)	12.5	13.7	16.5	18.2	12.7	2.7	1.6	1.5
Total foreign currency deposits/GDP (λ_D)	56.3	63.3	78.0	63.7	69.4	59.4	48.5	45.7
Nonresidents' foreign currency deposits/Total foreign currency deposits (S_{NR})	39.6	41.6	45.6	32.8	24.4	20.9	20.6	19.8
Residents' foreign currency deposits/Total foreign currency deposits (S_R)	60.4	58.4	54.4	67.2	75.6	79.1	79.4	80.2
Banks' liquid foreign assets as a share of foreign currency deposits-corrected (α^C)	16.2	17.3	13.9	21.4	28.9	41.0	42.8	37.3

Source: Central Bank of Uruguay.

Table 8.2. Fixed Parameters

Coverage of nonresidents' deposits (C_{NR})	100%
Coverage of residents' deposits (C_R)	30%
Accumulated output loss (γ)	14%
Probability of sudden stop (π)	7.5%
Term premium (δ)	1.5%
Risk-free rate (r)	5%
Risk aversion (σ)	2
Real exchange rate depreciation (Δq)	30%
Long-run GDP growth rate (g)	3%

Source: IMF staff assumptions.

ing in the magnitude of deposit withdrawals ($\varphi\lambda_D$), private (λ_P) and public (λ_G) short-term foreign currency debt, output cost (γ), and the likelihood of a crisis (π). Intuitively, reserves are more useful as a buffer: the larger the drop in consumption (caused by the withdrawal of dollar deposits and sudden stop in foreign currency credit) and the bigger the probability of such drop. A larger coverage of dollar deposits by banks' own reserve holdings (that is, by banks' liquid foreign assets[6]—$\alpha\lambda_D$) implies less optimal (official) reserves, because such coverage also cushions dollar deposit withdrawals in a crisis. In addition, a real exchange rate depreciation (Δq) increases the burden of foreign currency liabilities, leading to further drops in consumption and, thus, larger optimal reserves. Finally, the optimal level of reserves is decreasing in the cost of holding reserves, which is captured by the interest rate differential between long-term debt issued to finance reserves and the return on reserves (δ).

$$\rho = \lambda + \gamma + \frac{(1-\gamma)p^{1/\sigma}\Delta q}{1+[p^{1/\sigma}(1+\Delta q)-1](1-\pi-\delta)} - \frac{p^{1/\sigma}(1+\Delta q)-1}{1+[p^{1/\sigma}(1+\Delta q)-1](1-\pi-\delta)} \left\{1-\frac{r-g}{1+g}(\lambda+(1-\varphi)\lambda_D)-(\pi+\delta)(\lambda+\gamma)\right\}, \qquad (1)$$

where $\lambda = (\varphi-\alpha)\lambda_D + \lambda_P + \lambda_G$, $\varphi = s_R C_R + s_{NR} C_{NR}$, and

$$p = \frac{(1-\pi)(\delta+\pi)}{\pi(1-\delta-\pi)(1+\Delta q)}.$$

Although the ratio of liquid foreign assets of banks to foreign currency deposits has been relatively stable in Uruguay, the composition of foreign currency deposits has shifted from nonresidents to residents in recent years. Because, in the event of a crisis, the percentage drop in nonresidents' deposits is typically larger than for residents' deposits, the current coverage of deposits by banks' liquid foreign assets can be considered stronger than in 2002. To reflect this in the calibration, the model corrects the ratio of banks' liquid foreign assets

[6]Banks' liquid foreign currency assets comprise cash, bonds, and deposits with maturity of less than one year in a remaining maturity basis.

to dollar deposits to control for the change in residents/nonresidents composition of deposits over time.[7]

Many of the parameters are calibrated following standard conventions. The risk aversion parameter is set at 2, a number typically used in the business cycle literature. The risk-free short-term dollar interest rate (the return of reserves) is set to 5 percent, about the average U.S. three-month t-bill rates in the past 10 years. The term premium is assumed to be 1.5 percent, close to the average difference between the yield on 10-year U.S. treasury bonds and the federal funds rate in the past 20 years. The growth of potential output in Uruguay is calibrated at 3 percent. The real exchange rate depreciation following a crisis is calibrated at 30 percent, slightly less than the 33 percent depreciation that took place between March and September 2002.

Coverage of foreign currency deposits by official reserves and banks' liquid foreign assets was set at 100 percent for nonresidents and 30 percent for residents. The full coverage for nonresidents' deposits, which broadly matches the current practice by banks in Uruguay, would insulate the domestic economy from sudden withdrawals by nonresidents, which can be large as evidenced by the 2002 crisis. Because residents' deposits are less volatile than nonresidents', a smaller coverage of 30 percent seems appropriate.

The output loss owing to a crisis was calibrated at 7 percent of GDP per year during two years. The accumulated output loss of the Uruguayan economy as a result of the 2002 crisis was about 18.5 percent, and output took roughly two years to recover to its precrisis levels. Given the improved external conditions, compared with 2002 (when the devaluation in Brazil was followed by a severe crisis in Argentina), we assumed a smaller output loss (14 percent). This is also close to estimates found in the literature on currency crises and sudden stops for a typical emerging market country.[8]

The probability of a crisis was calibrated at 7.5 percent a year, or an average of one crisis every 15 years. The JR estimation, based on a cross-country probit model, yields a probability of 10 percent for a typical emerging market country. Nonetheless, Uruguay's track record of one major crisis every 20 years (1982 and 2002) implies an observed crisis frequency of 5 percent. Given the potential specification problems of the probit estimation and the difficulty of inferring the probability from Uruguay's few crisis episodes, the calibration is set to the intermediate probability of 7.5 percent.

As vulnerabilities have diminished since 2002, so has the estimated optimal level of reserves. Because short-term foreign currency indebtedness and deposit dollarization have been decreasing since 2002, and given the banks' exceptionally high liquidity levels, the need for central bank reserves for prudential purposes has diminished (Figure 8.5). Prior to the crisis, the estimated optimal level of reserves reached almost 80 percent of GDP in 2001 (or US$14.7 billion), highlighting the large vulnerabilities of the economy at the time. In June 2007, with fewer vulnerabilities, the optimal level of central bank reserves was estimated to be less than 20 percent of GDP (or around US$3.8 billion). That is about 1.7 percent of GDP (or US$300 million) above current levels.[9]

Simulations indicate that reserves are close to adequate levels and would be nearly sufficient to deal with a 2002-like crisis.[10] This is a consequence of increased reserves and, more important, reduced vulnerabilities. Figure 8.6 simulates the results of a 2002-like crisis, that is, drops in nonresidents' and residents' deposits and short-term debt of 63 percent, 36 percent, and 26 percent, respectively. Whereas such drops generated a severe reserve gap in 2002 in the absence of external support, a similar scenario in 2006 yields a much smaller gap.

However, further accumulation is still desirable. In particular, the optimal level of central bank reserves is likely to increase in the next few years, as the ongoing credit recovery matures and banks reduce their currently high holdings of liquid external assets. As an illustration of a relatively extreme scenario, Figure 8.5 shows that the optimal level of reserves as of June 2007 would increase to 28.9 percent of GDP (or about US$5.7 billion) if banks' coverage of deposits by own

---

[7]In the model, α is defined as the ratio of banks' liquid foreign assets (*BLFA*) to total dollar deposits (residents: *R*; nonresidents: *NR*), $\alpha = \frac{BLFA}{R+NR}$. Note that α can be rewritten as follows:

$$\alpha = \frac{BLFA}{R+NR} = \frac{BLFA}{NR} \times \frac{NR}{R+NR}.$$

The first term, the coverage of nonresidents' deposits by BLFA, has increased since the 2002 crisis, whereas the second term, the share of nonresidents' deposits, has decreased. The reduction of the latter term implies a reduction in the risk of large deposit withdrawals. For comparability purposes, it is sensible to maintain the same "level of risk" in all years of the sample. This is done by assuming that in previous years the composition of residents'/nonresidents' deposits was the same as in 2006, yielding the corrected measure

$$\alpha_y^C = \frac{BLFA}{R+NR} = \left(\frac{BLFA}{NR}\right)_y \times \left(\frac{NR}{R+NR}\right)_{2006},$$

where *y* is the year under consideration.

[8]Hutchison and Noy (2005) find that the cumulative output loss of a sudden stop (defined as a simultaneous occurrence of a currency/balance of payments crisis with a reversal in capital inflows) is about 13–15 percent of GDP.

[9]The definition of the actual level of reserves excludes an account of the government in the central bank that has liquid foreign assets. Although the value of assets in this account can be very large, it is also very volatile (in end-2005, it had US$328 million; then in end-2006, the account had zero assets; in June 2007, it had US$1.2 billion) and is not included in official reserve figures because it is typically held by the government momentarily and used for debt management purposes, not as precautionary reserves.

[10]See Appendix 8.2 for an explanation on how simulation results were obtained.

Figure 8.5. Optimal Versus Actual Level of Reserves in Uruguay
(In percent of GDP)

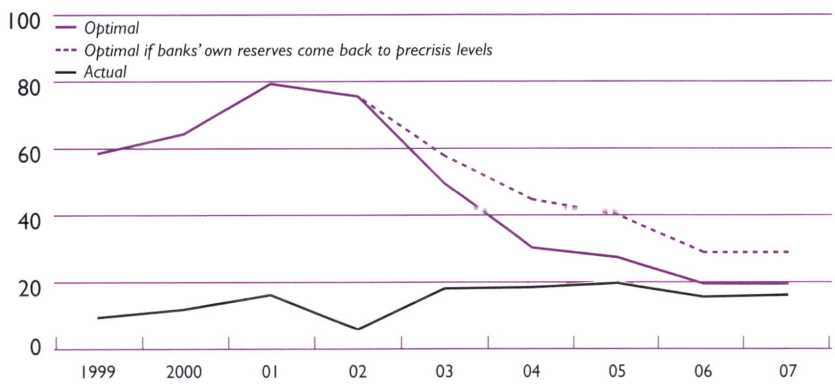

Source: IMF staff estimates.

Figure 8.6. Actual and Implied Reserves
(In percent of GDP)

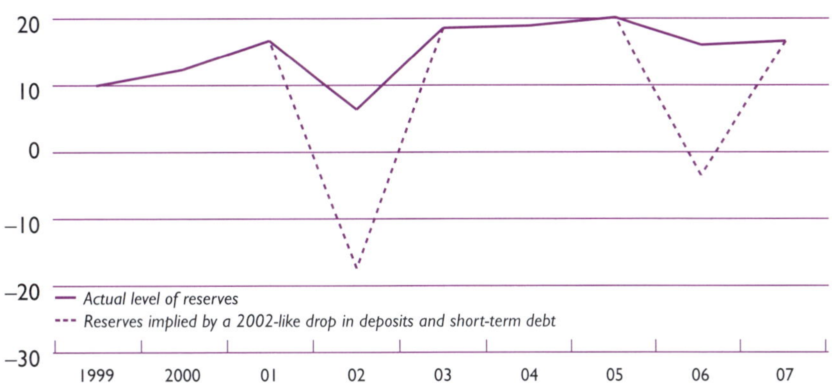

Sources: Central Bank of Uruguay; and IMF staff calculations.

foreign liquid assets returned to precrisis levels.[11] This highlights the importance of proper banking regulation that addresses the vulnerabilities caused by dollar deposits, thereby limiting the need for central bank reserve accumulation.

[11]The dashed line in Figure 8.5 assumes that the corrected ratio of banks' liquid assets to deposits is at a precrisis level (the latter is obtained by the 1999–2001 average of the ratio of banks' liquid assets to deposits).

Sensitivity Analysis

The optimal level of reserves is very sensitive to calibration choices. Thus, undertaking a sensitivity analysis is important to gain broader perspective on the results under different conditions or parameter values. Figure 8.7 focuses on those parameters that, if changed, most affect the optimal level of reserves. The following facts emerge: (1) an increase in short-term foreign currency debt to 25 percent of GDP (a level close to the

Figure 8.7. Sensitivity Analysis

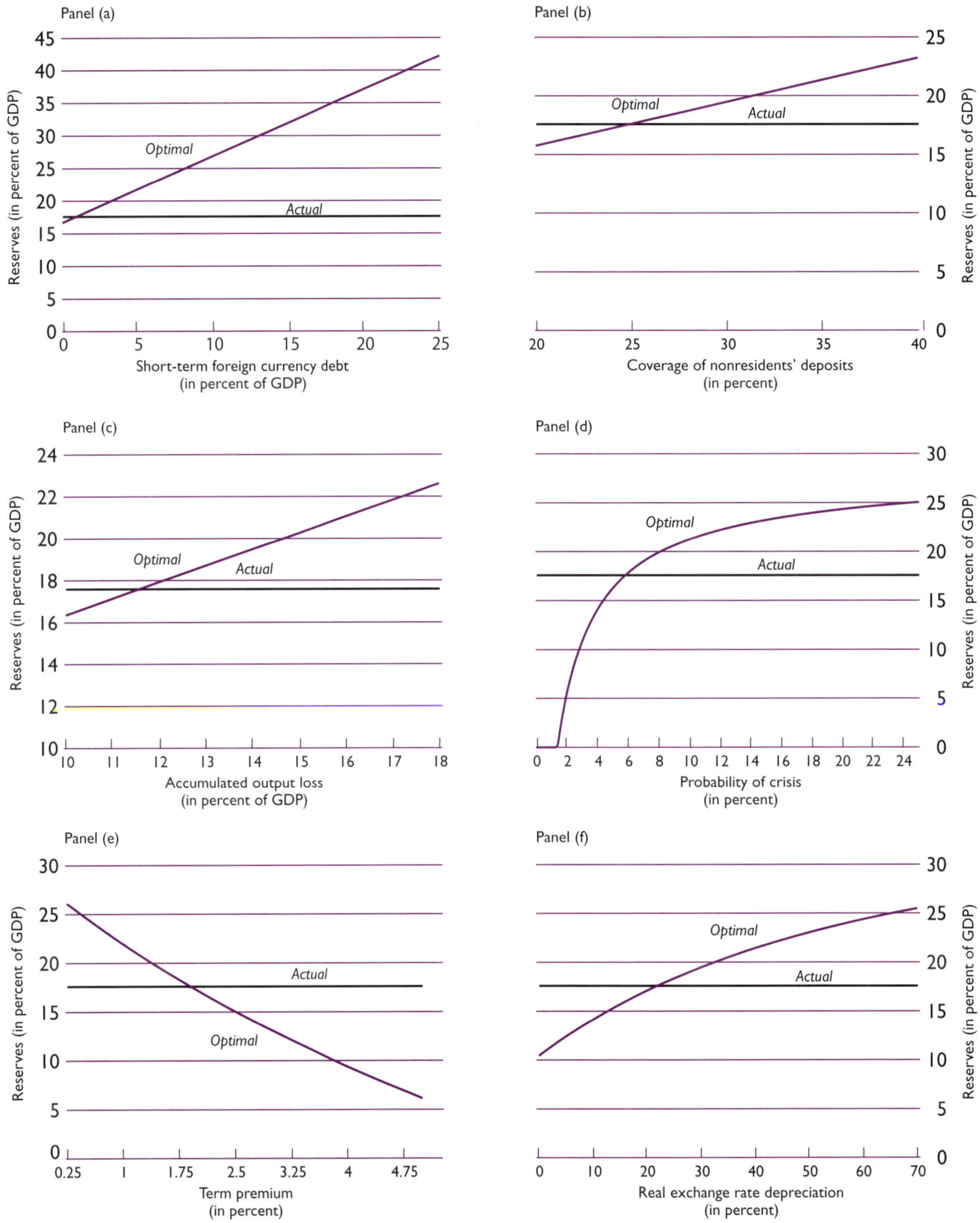

Source: Authors' calculations.

2001 level) would result in an optimal level of reserves of more than 40 percent of GDP; (2) coverage of residents' deposits in the range of 10–40 percent would imply reserve levels between 15 and 25 percent of GDP; (3) an output loss of the magnitude observed in 2002 (about 18.5 percent of GDP) would imply an optimal level of reserves of more than 22 percent of GDP; (4) the JR calibration of a 10 percent probability of a crisis would yield an optimal level of reserves of 21 percent of GDP; (5) an increase in the term premium from 1.5 to 2.5 percent would raise the cost of holding reserves, and would lead to a sharp drop in the optimal level of reserves (more than 4 percent of GDP); and (6) a real exchange rate depreciation between 0 and 70 percent results in optimal reserve levels between 10 and 25 percent of GDP.

The current reserve levels would be optimal under certain assumptions. For example, if the parameter on coverage of residents' foreign currency deposits were reduced from 30 percent to 25 percent of deposits, the model would suggest optimal reserves roughly in line with existing levels. An accumulated output loss of 11–12 percent (much smaller than the 2002 experience) or a probability of crisis just below 6 percent would yield similar results. Finally, a term premium of 2 percent (significantly higher than historical averages), or a real exchange rate depreciation in a crisis of about 22 percent (much smaller than observed in the last crisis), would also imply that the current reserve level is optimal (Table 8.3).

Table 8.3. Implicit Parameters
(In percent)

Short-term foreign currency debt/GDP ($\lambda_G+\lambda_P$)	0.9
Coverage of residents' deposits (C_R)	24.8
Accumulated output loss (γ)	11.6
Probability of sudden stop (π)	5.8
Term premium (δ)	2.0
Real exchange rate depreciation (Δq)	21.8

Source: IMF staff calculations and assumptions.

Conclusions

A model calibrated for Uruguay, a financially dollarized economy, suggests that reserves are nearing optimal prudential levels. The model takes into account the risk of financial account reversals typically analyzed in these studies and the possibility of large withdrawals of foreign currency deposits in the event of a crisis. With the substantial decline of nonresidents' deposits and short-term foreign currency debt since the 2002 crisis, and the high holdings of liquid foreign currency assets by banks, the prudential benefit of holding official reserves has diminished. In the model, this is reflected in a significant drop of the optimal level of reserves since 2002 that, together with the accumulation of reserves by the central bank, has nearly closed the gap between the optimal and the actual reserve levels.

Nonetheless, there are several reasons that justify further reserve accumulation. In particular, with banks' currently high liquidity levels unlikely to be permanent, the optimal level of official reserves should increase in the years ahead. Also, sensitivity analysis shows that an increase in short-term foreign currency indebtedness, among other possible changes in economic conditions, would lead to a large increase of the optimal level of reserves. In addition, with the model focusing on crisis mitigation (rather than crisis prevention), the calculated optimal level of reserves could be seen as a lower bound. By assuming a crisis probability independent of reserves, the model did not capture a possible preventive role of reserves (see García and Soto (2006); Jeanne (2007); and Chami, McGettigan, and Watt (2007)). Adding this role would provide another reason to hold reserves, most likely leading to an increase in the model predictions about optimal reserve levels.

Appendix 8.1. A Model of Optimal Reserve Levels in Financially Dollarized Economies

Consider a small open economy in discrete time that may be hit by a "sudden stop," defined as an exogenous loss of external credit. When a sudden stop hits the economy, (1) short-term external debt is not rolled over, (2) a significant fraction of foreign currency deposits is withdrawn from the banking sector, (3) output falls, and (4) a real depreciation occurs. The (nonfinancial) private sector is subject to the following budget constraint:

$$C_t = Y_t + q_t[B_t - (1+r_B)B_{t-1} + P_t - (1+r)P_{t-1} + Z_t], \quad \text{(A.1)}$$

where C_t is domestic consumption, Y_t is domestic output, q_t is the real exchange rate, B_t is the dollar short-term lending by banks to the private sector, P_t is the short-term external debt of the private sector, and Z_t is a transfer from the government. The interest rates r_B and r are constant. Consumers do not default on short-term external debt, so r is a risk-free interest rate. Banks are subject to the following budget constraint:

$$B_t - (1+r_B)B_{t-1} + RB_t - (1+r)RB_{t-1} = D_t - (1+r_D)D_{t-1}, \quad \text{(A.2)}$$

where RB_t is the amount of dollar deposits that banks invest in risk-free short-term foreign assets (in dollars) at an interest rate of r, and D_t represents dollar deposits for which banks pay an interest rate of r_D. RB_t is assumed to be a constant fraction of short-term foreign currency deposits: $RB_t = \alpha D_t$, $0<\alpha<1$.[12] Furthermore, for simplicity, $r_D = r$ (introducing a premium in domestic foreign currency deposits would not fundamentally alter our results).

As in JR, the government issues a long-term security that is sold by the price P (assumed constant), and yields one unit of good every period until the sudden stop occurs, after which it stops yielding any income. Therefore, the price of this security before the sudden stop occurs is given by the present discounted value of its expected future returns,

$$P = \frac{1}{1+r+\delta}[1+(1-\pi)P],$$

where π is the probability that a sudden stop occurs, r is the interest rate on short-term external debt, and δ is the term premium. Solving the expression above for P yields

$$P = \frac{1}{r+\delta+\pi}. \tag{A.3}$$

The long-term security is issued to finance a stock R_t of official reserves, implying that

$$R_t = PN_t, \tag{A.4}$$

where N_t is the number of long-term securities issued by the government in period t.

The government may also issue short-term foreign debt in non-sudden-stop periods. Therefore, before the sudden stop, government's budget constraint is given by

$$P(N_t - N_{t-1}) - N_{t-1} + G_t - (1+r)G_{t-1} = Z_t + R_t - (1+r)R_{t-1}, \tag{A.5}$$

where G_t is the short-term foreign debt of the government (the government does not default on its short-term external debt, implying that the interest rate on this debt is the risk-free interest rate, r).

The subscripts b and d denote the periods before and during a sudden stop. Equations (A.4) and (A.5) can be used to substitute out P, N_t, and N_{t-1} from the government's budget constraint, yielding the expression for the government transfer to the private sector before the sudden stop,

$$Z_t^b = G_t - (1+r)G_{t-1} - (\delta+\pi)R_{t-1}. \tag{A.6}$$

The third term in equation (A.6) corresponds to the cost of carrying reserves, which is proportional to the term premium plus a default risk premium, captured by the sudden stop probability. To pay for this cost, the government taxes the consumer, reducing the government transfer. When a sudden stop occurs, private and public short-term external debt can no longer be issued. To smooth the effects on consumption of the sudden stop of external credit, the government transfers its official reserves to consumers, except for the amount $(\delta+\pi)R_{t-1}$, which it has to pay on its long-run security for the last time. Therefore, transfers during a sudden stop are given by

$$Z_t^d = -(1+r)G_{t-1} + (1-\delta-\pi)R_{t-1}. \tag{A.7}$$

Assuming that $\delta+\pi<1$, the term $(1-\delta-\pi)R_{t-1}$ will be positive. In the long run, output grows at rate g. When the balance of payments crisis unfolds, a fraction of output is lost, and a fraction of dollar deposits φ is withdrawn from banks. Furthermore, the real exchange rate is constant and normalized to 1 before the crisis and depreciates by Δq during the crisis. With these assumptions and the equations for the transfer in (A.6) and (A.7), the expressions for domestic consumption before and during the crisis are, respectively,

$$C_t^b = Y_t^b + (1-\alpha)D_t^b + P_t^b + G_t^b - (1+r)\left[(1-\alpha)D_{t-1}^b + P_{t-1}^b + G_{t-1}^b\right] - (\delta+\pi)R_{t-1}; \tag{A.8}$$

$$C_t^d = (1-\gamma)Y_t^b + (1+\Delta q)\left\{(1-\varphi)D_{t-1}^b - (1+r)\left[(1-\alpha)D_{t-1}^b + P_{t-1}^b + G_{t-1}^b\right] + (1-\delta-\pi)R_{t-1}\right\}. \tag{A.9}$$

The government chooses the amount of reserves to maximize the expected welfare of consumers,

$$E(U_t) = E\left[\sum_{s=0}^{\infty}(1+r)^s u(C_{t+s})\right], \text{ where}$$

$$u(C) = \frac{C^{1-\sigma}-1}{1-\sigma}. \tag{A.10}$$

The first-order condition to this problem is

$$\pi\cdot(1-\delta-\pi)\cdot(1+\Delta q)\cdot u'(C_{t+1}^d) = (1-\pi)\cdot(\delta+\pi)\cdot u'(C_{t+1}^b). \tag{A.11}$$

From equation (A.11), it can be shown that the optimal level of reserves before the sudden stop is a constant fraction of output,

$$R_t = \rho Y_{t+1}^b, \tag{A.12}$$

where the optimal ratio of reserves to output ρ is given by equation (1) in the text.

[12]The model abstracts from moral hazard issues related to the fact that reserve accumulation by the central bank may cause banks to decide to hold fewer foreign currency assets. Levy Yeyati (2006) focuses on this issue and obtains an optimal composition of reserves between the banking sector and the central bank.

Appendix 8.2. Level of Reserves Required to Cover a 2002-Like Crisis

The total drop in short-term foreign currency deposits is the sum of the drop in nonresidents' deposits (ΔNR) and residents' deposits (ΔR) and can be written as follows:

$$\Delta D = \Delta NR + \Delta R = (NR+R)\left(\frac{NR}{NR+R}\frac{\Delta NR}{NR} + \frac{R}{NR+R}\frac{\Delta R}{R}\right) =$$

$$D\left(\frac{NR}{NR+R}\frac{\Delta NR}{NR} + \frac{R}{NR+R}\frac{\Delta R}{R}\right).$$

The drop in NR and R is calibrated based on the 2002 crisis, whereas the composition of deposits in terms of NR and R is obtained from actual data in each year. In other words, the drop in deposits in a particular year y is given by

$$\Delta D_y = D_y\left[\left(\frac{NR}{NR+R}\right)_y\left(\frac{\Delta NR}{NR}\right)_{2002} + \left(\frac{R}{NR+R}\right)_y\left(\frac{\Delta R}{R}\right)_{2002}\right]. \quad \text{(A.13)}$$

Similarly, the drop in short-term foreign currency debt (ΔL) can be written as $\Delta L = L(\Delta L/L)$, and the size of the drop is calibrated based on the 2002 crisis:

$$\Delta L_y = L_y(\Delta L/L)_{2002}. \quad \text{(A.14)}$$

The implied level of reserves is simply the level that would result if reserves were used to cover the fall in deposits and debt implied by equations (A.13) and (A.14). As a share of GDP, this would be

$$\rho_y = \frac{(\Delta Dy + \Delta Ly)}{GDP_y}, \quad \text{(A.15)}$$

where ρ_y is the actual level of reserves in year y.

Bibliography

Becker, Törbjörn, Olivier Jeanne, Paolo Mauro, Jonathan D. Ostry, and Romain Rancière, 2007, *Country Insurance: the Role of Domestic Policies*, IMF Occasional Paper No. 254 (Washington: International Monetary Fund).

Chami, Saade, Donal McGettigan, and Stanley Watt, 2007, "Jordan's International Reserve Position: Justifiably Strong," IMF Working Paper 07/103 (Washington: International Monetary Fund).

de la Plaza, Luis, and Sophie Sirtaine, 2005, "An Analysis of the 2002 Uruguayan Banking Crisis," Policy Research Paper No. 3780 (Washington: World Bank).

European Central Bank, 2006, "The Accumulation of Foreign Reserves," ECB Occasional Paper No. 43 (Frankfurt am Main).

García, Pablo S., and Claudio Soto, 2006, "Large Hoarding of International Reserves: Are They Worth It?" in *External Financial Vulnerability and Preventive Policies*, ed. by Ricardo Caballero, César Calderón, and Luis Céspedes (Santiago: Central Bank of Chile).

Hutchison, Michael M., and Ilan Noy, 2005, "How Bad Are Twins? Output Costs of Currency and Banking Crises," *Journal of Money, Credit and Banking*, Vol. 37 (August), pp. 725–52.

Jeanne, Olivier, 2007, "International Reserves in Emerging Market Countries: Too Much of a Good Thing?" *Brookings Papers on Economic Activity: 1*, Brookings Institution, pp. 1–80.

———, and Romain Rancière, 2006, "The Optimal Level of International Reserves for Emerging Market Countries: Formulas and Applications," IMF Working Paper 06/229 (Washington: International Monetary Fund).

Kamil, Herman, 2006, "Balance-Sheet Mismatches and Cross-Sectoral Vulnerabilities in a Highly Dollarized Economy: The Case of Uruguay," *Uruguay: Selected Issues*, IMF Country Report No. 06/427 (Washington: International Monetary Fund).

Levy Yeyati, Eduardo, 2006, "Liquidity Insurance in a Financially Dollarized Economy," NBER Working Paper No. 12345 (Cambridge, Massachusetts: National Bureau of Economic Research).

Wijnholds, J. Onno de Beaufort, and Arend Kapteyn, 2001, "Reserve Adequacy in Emerging Market Economies," IMF Working Paper 01/143 (Washington: International Monetary Fund).

Recent Occasional Papers of the International Monetary Fund

263. Macroeconomic Implications of Financial Dollarization: The Case of Uruguay, edited by Marco Piñón, Gaston Gelos, and Alejandro López-Mejía. 2008.
262. IMF Support and Crisis Prevention, by Atish Ghosh, Bikas Joshi, Jun Il Kim, Uma Ramakrishnan, Alun Thomas, and Juan Zalduendo. 2008.
261. Exchange Rate Assessments: CGER Methodologies, by Jaewoo Lee, Gian Maria Milesi-Ferretti, Jonathan D. Ostry, Luca Antonio Ricci, and Alessandro Prati. 2008.
260. Managing the Oil Revenue Boom: The Role of Fiscal Institutions, by Rolando Ossowski, Mauricio Villafuerte, Paulo A. Medas, and Theo Thomas. 2008.
259. Macroeconomic Consequences of Remittances, by Ralph Chami, Adolfo Barajas, Thomas Cosimano, Connel Fullenkamp, Michael Gapen, and Peter Montiel. 2008.
258. Northern Star: Canada's Path to Economic Prosperity, edited by Tamim Bayoumi, Vladimir Klyuev, and Martin Mühleisen. 2007.
257. Economic Growth and Integration in Central America, edited by Dominique Desruelle and Alfred Schipke. 2007.
256. Moving to Greater Exchange Rate Flexibility: Operational Aspects Based on Lessons from Detailed Country Experiences, by Inci Ötker-Robe and David Vávra, and a team of IMF economists. 2007.
255. Sovereign Debt Restructuring and Debt Sustainability: An Analysis of Recent Cross-Country Experience, by Harald Finger and Mauro Mecagni. 2007.
254. Country Insurance: The Role of Domestic Policies, by Törbjörn Becker, Olivier Jeanne, Paolo Mauro, Jonathan D. Ostry, and Romain Rancière. 2007.
253. The Macroeconomics of Scaling Up Aid: Lessons from Recent Experience, by Andrew Berg, Shekhar Aiyar, Mumtaz Hussain, Shaun Roache, Tokhir Mirzoev, and Amber Mahone. 2007.
252. Growth in the Central and Eastern European Countries of the European Union, by Susan Schadler, Ashoka Mody, Abdul Abiad, and Daniel Leigh. 2006.
251. The Design and Implementation of Deposit Insurance Systems, by David S. Hoelscher, Michael Taylor, and Ulrich H. Klueh. 2006.
250. Designing Monetary and Fiscal Policy in Low-Income Countries, by Abebe Aemro Selassie, Benedict Clements, Shamsuddin Tareq, Jan Kees Martijn, and Gabriel Di Bella. 2006.
249. Official Foreign Exchange Intervention, by Shogo Ishi, Jorge Iván Canales-Kriljenko, Roberto Guimarães, and Cem Karacadag. 2006.
248. Labor Market Performance in Transition: The Experience of Central and Eastern European Countries, by Jerald Schiff, Philippe Egoumé-Bossogo, Miho Ihara, Tetsuya Konuki, and Kornélia Krajnyák. 2006.
247. Rebuilding Fiscal Institutions in Post-Conflict Countries, by Sanjeev Gupta, Shamsuddin Tareq, Benedict Clements, Alex Segura-Ubiergo, Rina Bhattacharya, and Todd Mattina. 2005.
246. Experience with Large Fiscal Adjustments, by George C. Tsibouris, Mark A. Horton, Mark J. Flanagan, and Wojciech S. Maliszewski. 2005.
245. Budget System Reform in Emerging Economies: The Challenges and the Reform Agenda, by Jack Diamond. 2005.
244. Monetary Policy Implementation at Different Stages of Market Development, by a staff team led by Bernard J. Laurens. 2005.
243. Central America: Global Integration and Regional Cooperation, edited by Markus Rodlauer and Alfred Schipke. 2005.
242. Turkey at the Crossroads: From Crisis Resolution to EU Accession, by a staff team led by Reza Moghadam. 2005.
241. The Design of IMF-Supported Programs, by Atish Ghosh, Charis Christofides, Jun Kim, Laura Papi, Uma Ramakrishnan, Alun Thomas, and Juan Zalduendo. 2005.
240. Debt-Related Vulnerabilities and Financial Crises: An Application of the Balance Sheet Approach to Emerging Market Countries, by Christoph Rosenberg, Ioannis Halikias, Brett House, Christian Keller, Jens Nystedt, Alexander Pitt, and Brad Setser. 2005.

239. GEM: A New International Macroeconomic Model, by Tamim Bayoumi, with assistance from Douglas Laxton, Hamid Faruqee, Benjamin Hunt, Philippe Karam, Jaewoo Lee, Alessandro Rebucci, and Ivan Tchakarov. 2004.

238. Stabilization and Reforms in Latin America: A Macroeconomic Perspective on the Experience Since the Early 1990s, by Anoop Singh, Agnès Belaisch, Charles Collyns, Paula De Masi, Reva Krieger, Guy Meredith, and Robert Rennhack. 2005.

237. Sovereign Debt Structure for Crisis Prevention, by Eduardo Borensztein, Marcos Chamon, Olivier Jeanne, Paolo Mauro, and Jeromin Zettelmeyer. 2004.

236. Lessons from the Crisis in Argentina, by Christina Daseking, Atish R. Ghosh, Alun Thomas, and Timothy Lane. 2004.

235. A New Look at Exchange Rate Volatility and Trade Flows, by Peter B. Clark, Natalia Tamirisa, and Shang-Jin Wei, with Azim Sadikov and Li Zeng. 2004.

234. Adopting the Euro in Central Europe: Challenges of the Next Step in European Integration, by Susan M. Schadler, Paulo F. Drummond, Louis Kuijs, Zuzana Murgasova, and Rachel N. van Elkan. 2004.

233. Germany's Three-Pillar Banking System: Cross-Country Perspectives in Europe, by Allan Brunner, Jörg Decressin, Daniel Hardy, and Beata Kudela. 2004.

232. China's Growth and Integration into the World Economy: Prospects and Challenges, edited by Eswar Prasad. 2004.

231. Chile: Policies and Institutions Underpinning Stability and Growth, by Eliot Kalter, Steven Phillips, Marco A. Espinosa-Vega, Rodolfo Luzio, Mauricio Villafuerte, and Manmohan Singh. 2004.

230. Financial Stability in Dollarized Countries, by Anne-Marie Gulde, David Hoelscher, Alain Ize, David Marston, and Gianni De Nicolò. 2004.

229. Evolution and Performance of Exchange Rate Regimes, by Kenneth S. Rogoff, Aasim M. Husain, Ashoka Mody, Robin Brooks, and Nienke Oomes. 2004.

228. Capital Markets and Financial Intermediation in The Baltics, by Alfred Schipke, Christian Beddies, Susan M. George, and Niamh Sheridan. 2004.

227. U.S. Fiscal Policies and Priorities for Long-Run Sustainability, edited by Martin Mühleisen and Christopher Towe. 2004.

226. Hong Kong SAR: Meeting the Challenges of Integration with the Mainland, edited by Eswar Prasad, with contributions from Jorge Chan-Lau, Dora Iakova, William Lee, Hong Liang, Ida Liu, Papa N'Diaye, and Tao Wang. 2004.

225. Rules-Based Fiscal Policy in France, Germany, Italy, and Spain, by Teresa Dában, Enrica Detragiache, Gabriel di Bella, Gian Maria Milesi-Ferretti, and Steven Symansky. 2003.

224. Managing Systemic Banking Crises, by a staff team led by David S. Hoelscher and Marc Quintyn. 2003.

223. Monetary Union Among Member Countries of the Gulf Cooperation Council, by a staff team led by Ugo Fasano. 2003.

222. Informal Funds Transfer Systems: An Analysis of the Informal Hawala System, by Mohammed El Qorchi, Samuel Munzele Maimbo, and John F. Wilson. 2003.

221. Deflation: Determinants, Risks, and Policy Options, by Manmohan S. Kumar. 2003.

220. Effects of Financial Globalization on Developing Countries: Some Empirical Evidence, by Eswar S. Prasad, Kenneth Rogoff, Shang-Jin Wei, and Ayhan Kose. 2003.

219. Economic Policy in a Highly Dollarized Economy: The Case of Cambodia, by Mario de Zamaroczy and Sopanha Sa. 2003.

218. Fiscal Vulnerability and Financial Crises in Emerging Market Economies, by Richard Hemming, Michael Kell, and Axel Schimmelpfennig. 2003.

217. Managing Financial Crises: Recent Experience and Lessons for Latin America, edited by Charles Collyns and G. Russell Kincaid. 2003.

Note: For information on the titles and availability of Occasional Papers not listed, please consult the IMF's *Publications Catalog* or contact IMF Publication Services.